Taunton's

2ND EDITION

TILING COMPLETE

EXPERT ADVICE FROM START TO FINISH

The Taunton Press

The Taunton Press, Inc.

63 South Main Street

Newtown, CT 06470-2344

e-mail: tp@taunton.com

Editors: Helen Albert, Sandor Nagyszalanczy, and Peter Chapman

Copy editor: Nina Rynd Whitnah

Indexer: Barbara Mortenson

Jacket/Cover design: Kimberly Adis

Interior design: Kimberly Adis

Layout: Cathy Cassidy and Barbara Cottingham

Illustrator: Trevor Johnston

Photographer: Sandor Nagyszalanczy, except Robin Nicholas and Michael Schweit p. 93 (top left, top right), pp. 254-256;

Courtesy Hoover, p. 244 (center bottom)

Library of Congress Cataloging-in-Publication Data

Names: Nicholas, Robin, author. | Schweit, Michael, author.

Title: Tiling complete : expert advice from start to finish / Robin Nicholas
   and Michael Schweit.

Other titles: Taunton's tiling complete

Description: 2nd edition. | Newtown, CT : The Taunton Press, Inc., [2018] |
   Previous edition: Taunton's tiling complete : expert advice from start to
   finish / Michael Schweit and Robin Nicholas. | Includes index.

Identifiers: LCCN 2017033566 | ISBN 9781641551984 (print) | ISBN 9781631869662 (pdf format) | ISBN 9781631869686 (mobi format)

Subjects: LCSH: Tile laying--Amateurs' manuals. | Tiles--Amateurs' manuals.

Classification: LCC TH8531 .S48 2018 | DDC 693/.3--dc23

LC record available at https://lccn.loc.gov/2017033566

Printed in the United States of America

10 9 8 7 6 5 4 3 2 1

The following manufacturers/names appearing in *Tiling Complete* are trademarks: Acrylbond®, AcrylPro®, Admix®, Ajax®, Bedrock® Industries, Bon Ami®, Bright Glaze®, Comet®, Custom Building Products®, Decora®, DensShield®, Dremel®, Dustbuster®, Grout Grabber®, Hardiboard®, Hoover® React™, James Hardie® Company, Masonite®, Miracle Sealants®, Nitrile®, Nuheat®, Ram Board®, RedGard®, RotoZip®, Schluter® system, SpeedSet™, TEC™, Tile Council of North America®, Triple Flex™, UltraGlasTiles®, Wedi®, Windex®, WonderBoard®, ZipWall®.

Construction is inherently dangerous. Using hand or power tools improperly or ignoring safety practices can lead to permanent injury or even death. Don't try to perform operations you learn about here (or elsewhere) unless you're certain they are safe for you. If something about an operation doesn't feel right, don't do it. Look for another way. We want you to enjoy working on your home, so please keep safety foremost in your mind whenever you're in the shop.

ACKNOWLEDGMENTS

Tile is the earthy material that has shaped our professional lives for many years and kept us connected to our world in incalculable ways. And it has also connected us to a multitude of wonderful people, many whose help was indispensable to our writing and production of this book.

As with the original edition of this book, our appreciation first goes to Sandor Nagyszalanczy for all of his time, effort, and winning photography. Sandor also gave us that important introduction to the Taunton Press and Helen Albert who saw the book through its first inception. We also honor our memories of Maria and Lorant Nagyszalanczy for their many kindnesses and generous access to their home.

In this new edition, we give special thanks to Peter Chapman for literally having his hand on the book for the first edition, and in the book at the outset of the new edition: for his willingness to work with us, for his superb editing skills, and for the phone camaraderie.

We'd also like to thank every person that helped this book come together, now and then, as well as many amiable dogs along the way and most notably, in memory of Molly. The comedic, emotional, and intellectual support of our families, friends, and a number of tile professionals buoyed us throughout this project, and we wish our text allowance would permit us to name each of you.

Our local tile establishments and their employees were exceptional in their assistance and cooperation. Joe Carey and Angel Arias of Tile Shop and all of their employees went above and beyond anything that was necessary for our needs during our time at their store/warehouse. Our appreciation for additional help goes to Warren Sehter and Bob Stiller at Trans World tile, and also to Westside Tile.

We've worked with many wonderful clients who graciously allowed us the use of their homes for some of the great photos in this book: Herb of Los Angeles, Lisa of Sherman Oaks, Jana Donnell-Spiegel and Philip Spiegel of Sherman Oaks, and Linda/David Schlossberg of Granada Hills.

We appreciated indispensable technical advice by L.J. and John Alldredge at Custom Building Products, Josh Bunch of Levelingspacers.com, Domenico Borrelli of Progress Profiles America Inc., Joel Beaton of WaleTale.net, Nuheat, Dave Stiles of Schluter Systems, and especially Mary Cordaro of Mary Cordaro, Inc.

—Robin Nicholas and Michael Schweit

GROUTING, CAULKING & SEALING 212

MAINTENANCE & REPAIR 242

INTRODUCTION

*T*iling Complete, the revised edition, contains information on how to design your project, how to purchase materials, which tools to buy, how to demolish and
prepare the area to be tiled by creating plumb and level
surfaces, how to tile counters and backsplashes, the ins
and outs of grouting, and how to repair and maintain
tile. We will lead you from start to completion, allay
your concerns, and enable you to tile just about any
area—except those that have high water use and exterior
projects. For those situations, the skills and experience
required go beyond the scope of this book.

Ten years ago, when we wrote the first edition of
this book, we were excited to share our enthusiasm for
ceramic tiles and impart our methods of installation
based on our many years of experience in residential
tile installations. In this updated and improved edition of
Tiling Complete, we illustrate new processes and techniques to show you how to utilize many of the current
tiles and enlist the appropriate methods of installation.

So what's new in the ensuing years since we wrote the
first edition? The BIGGEST change in the industry is the
introduction of BIG TILES! These tiles, otherwise known
as large-format tiles (anywhere from 15 in. all the way to
tiles that are larger than people), along with wood-look
plank tiles, create broad expanses of color and textures
with less grout, making them more similar to slab materials but requiring extra steps to lay them properly.

Additionally, we show you how to repair your tile after
some common plumbing repairs and how to install a
heated floor mat underneath your tile floor.

Another important inclusion is the use of epoxy grout.
Epoxy grout products have improved so much in the
ensuing time span that we encourage their use in more

applications than ever. Why not use a grout that is virtually stain proof and more durable?!

As we mentioned, tile sizes have changed; in addition,
colors, patterns, and textures alter and yet, they all
require a flawless installation, which is why most of the
information remains accurate and relevant. There are
some wonderful new edge trims and graphic tiles that
have even come around again, but staying current on
the apt installation method for your project will never go
out of style.

As with the first edition of the book, we will not show
you how to tile a water area such as a shower or a tub
surround. For even though a doctor could write a book
about how to remove your appendix, it is not something
you would or should attempt on your own. Tiling, like
any trade, has an important licensing process (in most
states) to ensure that the tradesperson you hire has
skills and knowledge, and that these tools allow them
to protect your home from damage from an improper
installation. Unfortunately, wet areas like showers and
tub surrounds can have inadequate or incorrect installations that may look good but whose problems will not be
revealed until the water seepage finally causes so much
damage that the work must be torn out.

Lastly, we have also omitted tiling exterior areas. With
all the considerations of exposure to sun or frost, proper
drainage, and correct placement of expansion joints, the
risks are too great for a failed installation.

In the end, whether you choose to install your tile
yourself or hire a professional, we hope this newest edition of *Tiling Complete* will help you feel more confident
whichever way you choose to make your tile dreams
come true.

STANDARD CERAMIC TILE

Commonly referred to by tile professionals as "white-bodied tile" (the glaze color covers the top surface of a tile that's all white inside), standard ceramic tile was once about the only tile you could get for home installations. It was mass-produced as 4-in. and 6-in. squares in a very limited number of colors (the grout used with it was typically white).

Today, there are many more color and shape options for standard ceramic tile. Because it is a relatively soft tile that chips and scratches easily, we generally reserve standard ceramic for use on bathroom vanities, tub enclosures, and other areas where it won't be subjected to heavy use. But this tile is very affordable and easy to work with, so standard ceramic is still a reasonable choice for kitchen countertops and backsplashes, especially if you're on a strict budget or if you're matching older ceramic tile in your home.

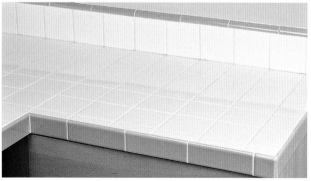

Standard ceramic tile **comes in a wide variety of solid colors as well as in decorative patterns.**

Tile terminology
Whether you're venturing into a tile store or talking to a tile contractor, it's good to know some tile terminology so you can talk the talk. Here are some common tile-related terms you're apt to hear when discussing or reading about tile:

Ceramic
Tile made from clay, then fired in a kiln. Its surface may be glazed or unglazed.

Bisque
A clay and liquid mixture that's combined and fired to make up the body of a tile.

Extruded
Tile trim or decorative shapes that are forced through a metal die to give them their shape before they are fired in a kiln.

Full body
Also called "through body." Porcelain tiles with color that's the same on the surface and all the way through the body of the tile.

Glazed
A mixture of liquid materials that is applied before firing to impart a hard, nonporous coating on the face of the tile. Usually colored and sometimes decorative.

Honed
Stone tile that has been ground to a smooth, matte surface finish.

Tumbled
Stone that has been tumbled in a drum with aggregates and sometimes chemicals to give it an aged, weathered appearance.

Vitreous
High-fired tile that's very dense and extremely resistant to water absorption, making it a good candidate for wet locations (bathrooms, laundry rooms) and outdoor applications.

White bodied
Any type of ceramic tile that's made up of a white clay body topped with a colored glaze.

PORCELAIN

Porcelain is very durable, **making it an excellent tile for flooring.**

Ersatz stone tiles made of porcelain come in a wide array of colors.

Full-body tiles **have the color throughout. Scratches won't show as they would on surface glazed tile.**

Porcelain is the right tile for kitchen countertops and high-use flooring. It's a bit more expensive than standard ceramic but makes up for the cost in durability because it wears very well in high-traffic areas. Porcelain tiles come in dozens of different finishes and colors, including ersatz stone tiles made to resemble many different types of stone. These "stone" porcelain tiles are a good choice if you like the look of stone but don't want to deal with the color and pattern variation of natural varieties.

Some porcelain tiles are "full-body" or "through-body" tiles, referring to the fact that the surface color runs throughout the body of the tile. This is an added bonus if you ever happen to scratch or chip a tile as the damage will not be very noticeable. If you choose porcelain tile for your project, make sure to check on the availability of trim because some porcelain tile lines have limited trim options. Also be aware that there are special requirements for setting porcelain tiles properly. These tiles can also be hard to cut cleanly, so you'll need to rent or buy a water saw.

TERRA-COTTA PAVERS

Terra-cotta **comes in different shapes and sizes and has slight color variations.**

M ade from natural clay, terra-cotta pavers have a soft body and a distinct earthy look that's all their own. Also known as "Saltillos," after the state of Saltillo in Coahuila, Mexico, where one type of this tile is hand-made, terra-cotta pavers work well in Southwestern or Spanish-colonial style homes. Many types are economical, but they do require the extra step of sealing.

Sometimes, handmade pavers will feature animal prints (thought to be good luck in Mexico). In contrast to more rustic-looking handmade Saltillos, machine-made terra-cotta pavers are much more uniform in color and size, creating a clean, more sophisticated look for modern homes. Terra-cotta pavers are available as presealed tiles that don't need to be top coated after installation. But many people prefer to buy unsealed tiles and apply their own finish, which can be matte or shiny. Unsealed terra-cotta can also be stained to give it a lighter off-white or darker brown color, as desired.

Features, such as paw prints, **add to the rustic, natural look of Saltillos.**

NATURAL STONE

Some years ago, if you wanted a natural stone floor in your home, you had to hire a skilled mason, who took random slabs of natural stone straight from the quarry and transformed them into a clean and elegant tile installation. Now, natural stone is readily available already cut, sized, and polished into tiles that any competent DIYer can install using the methods described in this book.

Several types of natural stone are available in tile form, including marble, travertine, limestone, slate, and granite. Each has its own range of colors and characteristic patterns and properties, as detailed in the sections that follow. Stone tiles come with either a polished, honed, or tumbled finish. Polished stone has a mirror-like surface that looks elegant and refined, but it tends to show scratches and wear. Honed stone has been ground to a matte surface, giving it a contemporary look that can also be used in traditional settings. Tumbled stone has a rough, pitted appearance that's more appropriate for a rustic tile design. The matte surface of tumbled stone doesn't show scratches or wear readily, but it tends to stain a bit easier than polished stone.

There are a few important things to consider before choosing natural stone for your project. (1) You'll need a tile saw to cut stone tiles to fit your installation. (2) Trim pieces (quarter-round, bullnose) are generally not available for stone tile. To create trim pieces, you'll need to purchase a stone-polishing and grinding kit or contact a stone fabricator. (3) Stone tiles require regular cleaning and maintenance, including periodic resealing, to keep them looking good. (4) Since stone is a product of nature, tiles can vary considerably in color and pattern. Some people love this natural variation. If you like stone but want a more consistent look, consider choosing faux stone tiles.

>> >> >>

A colorful selection of natural stone tiles.

Natural stone tiles like marble, travertine, slate, and limestone come tumbled, honed, or polished.

Travertine's rustic surface provides a look of antiquity.

NATURAL STONE (CONTINUED)

The color variations **among different marbles offer you many options in design.**

Marble

Marble is a soft stone with distinct patterns of colored veins that can give an installation an elegant, classic look. Colors range from white to black with just about every color in between. Due to its reactive nature with any acidic liquids, such as lemon or vinegar, marble is not a good choice for kitchen counters and food-preparation areas. Also, water spots can leave light mineral deposits, especially on polished marble surfaces.

Travertine

Imported from all over the world, travertine stone comes in mostly beige to gray tones. The surface of this sedimentary stone contains cavities that can hold dirt. For smoother, easier-to-clean tiles, you can either fill the surface cavities with grout or buy tiles that are prefilled with color-matched epoxy. Travertine is not a great choice for countertops, as acids such as lemon juice can etch the surface of the tile. Prices of this tile are wide ranging, reflecting the quality of the material; less expensive prefilled tiles often have vast areas of featureless epoxy; buy higher quality travertine for a richer, more natural appearance.

Limestone

Limestone is a naturally light stone, in colors ranging from beige to blue to gray. Some limestones show only mild shade variation from tile to tile; others display extreme variation (see "Variations in Natural Stone" on the facing page). The hardness of the limestone depends on where it was quarried. Limestone lacks travertine's characteristic pits and depressions, but some varieties show interesting features, including seashells and fossils. All stone tiles require maintenance, but most limestones require a bit more attention due to their susceptibility to staining and scratching. Limestone is not the best wearing tile, so avoid its use in high-traffic areas such as entries and kitchens.

Varied marble tiles are cut and preset on an adhesive sheet to give a 3-D effect on a backsplash or wall.

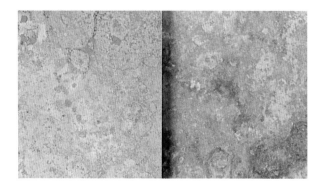

Travertine's tones make it a good choice for a neutral color scheme.

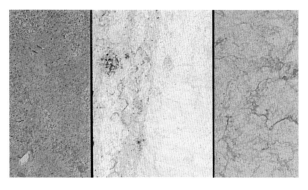

Limestone occasionally shows fossils. It's a soft stone and not well suited to high-traffic areas.

Slate

Slate is a natural stone found in a variety of earth tones, depending on its place of origin (India, China, Africa). Slate tiles come in two forms: "Calibrated" tiles are machine ground flat on both sides; "gauged" tiles are ground on the bottom, but the upper side is left with a natural, irregular surface. Often used on floors and sometimes on countertops, gauged slate tiles can elicit a rustic, outdoorsy look (it does have a tendency to "shed" very small pieces of stone over time, but this does not have an effect on the longevity of the installation). Conversely, calibrated slate can be used effectively in modern, minimalist decors. If you plan to use slate on a high-traffic floor, be sure to buy a high-quality slate (don't buy the bargain tile at 99¢ per square foot).

Granite

One of the hardest natural stone material you can find in the form of tile, granite has a wide range of colors, including grays, greens, reds, browns, and blacks. Granite tiles often have characteristic crystal-like features and veining, which can vary considerably from tile to tile. Highly resistant to scratches and stains, it is a good choice for floors and high-wear surfaces. However, if used on kitchen counters, granite tiles must be sealed to prevent food oils and fats from penetrating the surface and leaving blotchy stains.

>> >> >>

The earthy look of slate is perfect for a rustic room.

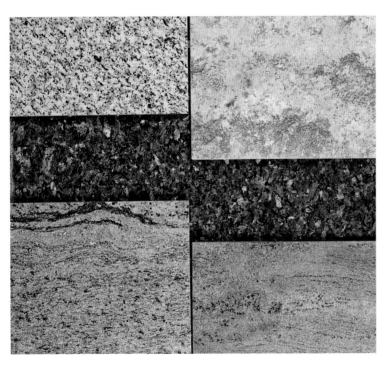

Granite is hard and resistant to scratches but must be sealed to prevent stains.

VARIATIONS IN NATURAL STONE

Stone tiles can vary considerably from one to the other. To help you visualize how variations in a particular kind of stone's color and pattern will look across your entire counter or floor, take a single tile and divide it into a grid of squares using narrow tape (available from an art supply store). Imagine that each small square represents an individual tile, and you'll get a preview of how an installation's worth of full-size tiles might look. If you don't like what you see, you probably won't want to choose that tile for your project.

NATURAL STONE (CONTINUED)

LEDGER STONE

Stacked stone ledger panels are trimmed pieces of natural stone that are glued together on the back to form modular stone veneer panels. They come in many different colors, stones, and sizes. Setting these panels on a wall surface is very straightforward, which makes this an excellent DIY project. Just keep in mind that you still want to keep the panels level as you work on your wall.

You can cut the panels with a wet saw or a dry cutting wheel on a handheld grinder. Match your thinset color to the stone because some may show through where the panels intersect. You can also purchase corners or create interlocking ones yourself.

Easy-to-install ledger stone panels **are growing in popularity. The panels are comparable in price to full-size solid stone.**

Some lines carry **premade stone corners or you can interlock them as shown.**

Ledger stone panels **and a travertine hearth enhance this fireplace with color, texture, and dimension.**

GLASS TILE

Some glass tiles **have embedded plant material or other decorative additions.**

Jewel-like glass **tile comes in a wide variety of sizes, shapes, and surface textures.**

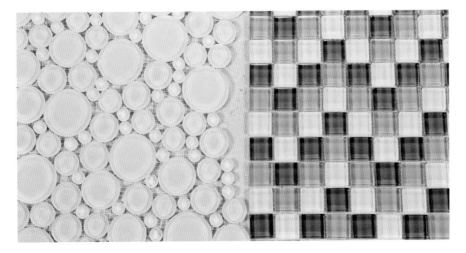

Glass tiles are available in a plethora of unusual shapes, **sizes, and colors, including these bubble shapes and multicolored rectangles. The two examples shown here are preset on netting, which allows them to lie well on any wall surface.**

Although glass tile has been around for a very long time, it has only recently been reinvented and now comes in many new forms and colors suitable for modern installations. Today, you can find all kinds of decorative and unusual glass tiles, including iridescent and glitter glass, tiles made from recycled wine bottles, and even clear tiles with imbedded flowers and a floral scent. Many kinds of glass tile have a translucency and/or shininess that can give your project an extra dimension and reflective highlights.

Most glass tiles are too fragile to use on countertops, floors, and other high-use surfaces (the exceptions are UltraGlasTiles® and Bedrock® Industries glass tiles which are rated for floor installation). Applied to a backsplash, glass tile can create a very classy look in a kitchen or bar. These tiles are a bit trickier to install than clay-based tiles due to their transparency and expansion and contraction properties. Glass tiles tend to be more expensive than clay-based tiles, but if you like the look, it's *clearly* worth it. If using glass tiles for your entire project breaks your budget, you might try using only a few of them as decorative accents.   >> >> >>

TRADE SECRET

If you fall in love with an exorbitantly expensive glass mosaic tile or beautiful decorative border, try pairing it with inexpensive standard ceramic tiles to help the project stay within your budget.

GLASS TILE (CONTINUED)

Setting large glass tile

Large glass tile can telegraph any debris left under the tile. Even trowel ridges can show through. Make sure to clean dust and dirt from the back of the tiles (whether or not the tiles have a coating on the underside), so that it won't show through when the tile is set **1**. Individual glass tiles larger than 4 sq. in. or glass trim tiles, including liners and accents, should be thinly back-buttered before they're set **2**. This prevents air pockets, voids, and notch marks from showing through, and ensures that the tiles are fully bonded to the substrate.

Glass tile larger than **4 sq. in. will show trowel ridges. Back-butter instead.**

1 Always clean glass tiles because dust and dirt can show through.

2 A thin, evenly applied layer of thinset on the back of a glass tile prevents voids and air pockets from forming when the tile is set.

SETTING FACE-MOUNTED GLASS TILE

1 After setting the tile, dampen the paper surface with a wet sponge.

2 After about 15 minutes, peel back a corner of the wet paper and lift it off the glass tile.

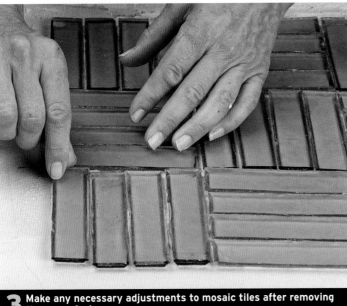

3 Make any necessary adjustments to mosaic tiles after removing the paper facing.

4 Clean any remaining residue from the tile the next day by rubbing with a damp sponge.

Setting face-mounted glass tile

Some kinds of small glass tiles come face mounted, with brown paper attached to the finish side with water-soluble glue. Spread thinset for these tiles as usual, then apply the tiles with the nonpaper side down. After the tile has been in place for a few hours, wet down the face-mounted paper with a damp sponge, allowing the water to penetrate the paper **1**. After about 15 minutes, try lifting a corner of the paper to see if it peels off easily. If it does, peel the paper off carefully **2**. If not, add some more water, wait another 15 minutes, and try again. After the paper has been removed, carefully adjust any tiles that have moved out of alignment **3**. After the thinset has dried overnight, use a damp sponge to remove any remaining paper or adhesive **4**.

SPECIALTY TILE

Mosaic tile **often comes mounted on mesh, making it easy to install.**

A mosaic border **creates an attractive detail for a backsplash or bath.**

An expanse of tile can be made much more interesting with the addition of decorative elements or unusual tile. Feeling bold? Do your entire backsplash in metal tile or mosaic tile.

Mosaic tile

Defined as being 2 in. or less in size, mosaic tiles can be made of standard ceramic, stone, even glass. These small tiles are usually sheet mounted on a paper or mesh backing, allowing you to lay many tiles at a time (much faster than laying each tiny tile individually). Mosaics come in an amazing range of colors, designs, and materials.

Some mosaics are made up of uniform tiles all of the same color, whereas others contain tiles of many colors and shapes that fit together like a jigsaw puzzle to create a pattern or picture. Such complex mosaics can add a nice visual focus to an otherwise plain installation—for example, a floor medallion in the middle of an entryway or hall. Patterned mosaic borders (preassembled on a backing) are also a great way to add accents to tiled backsplashes, walls, or counters.

This floor medallion **would add dramatic focus to any room.**

Decorative tiles can be sophisticated or fanciful.

Decorative tile

A decorative tile can be any sort of tile with a figurative or decorative pattern or design. Also known as "decos," some of these tiles have designs rendered as incised or raised surface relief. Other decos are adorned with colorful graphics, hand-painted images, pictures, or a combination of elements, including other materials. Small square or star-shape decos, known as "tacos," are made to add color to surfaces laid with octagonal tiles. And you can even commission personalized deco tiles, with, for example, painted or photo-realistic images.

Although they can be quite expensive, adding just a few decorative tiles to a plain tiled surface can effectively add a splash of color or some visual interest. Decos are also useful for defining or reinforcing a room's theme or design scheme.

>> >> >>

Many decorative tiles have embossed surfaces and must be masked during grouting.

SPECIALTY TILE (CONTINUED)

Metal tile

Some metal tiles are made entirely of metal, but most are cast from a bisque or other ceramic material that is then covered with a veneer of bronze, brass, copper, nickel, or other metal. Some tiles have designs rendered in surface relief, while others have etched patterns or embedded glass or ceramic elements. Rarely used to cover an entire surface, metal tiles are usually placed in combination with other kinds of tile to add a decorative accent that lends a striking or sophisticated look to a tile job. They look particularly good when used with light limestone or terra-cotta tiles. We paired inexpensive white ceramic tile with metal tiles to create a finish that complemented the chrome fixtures of a client's bathroom to great effect.

Like glass, metal tile is a bad choice on a floor or other heavy-use areas; most metal tiles are plated or coated, and these coatings wear off. Cutting metal tile requires some metalworking tools and skills.

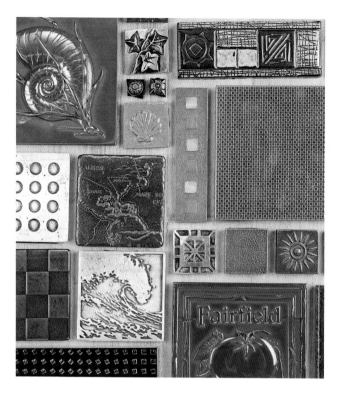

Metal tiles **add an exotic touch to an installation but can be expensive.**

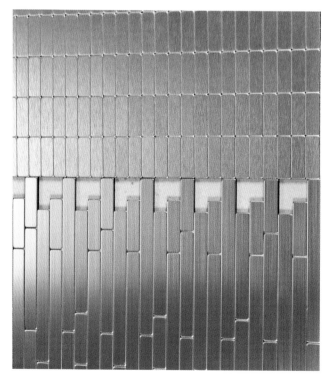

These metal tiles **are preset on sheets with their own adhesive. You just peel and stick them onto any flat wall surface and then grout.**

Wood-look plank tiles

Tile flooring has long been a great option for those who desire freedom from the dust and dirt of carpeted floors and appreciate the resiliency of ceramic tiles. Now there's also a solution for people who love the natural beauty of wood but not the maintenance that wood floors require. Wood-look plank tiles are a welcome practical choice because they won't scratch or stain and they come in a seemingly endless variety of sizes, colors, textures, and patterns. Many of these tiles are a very accurate representation of wood, down to the bark, knots, and growth rings. Others have subtle, calm patterns to provide a clean, relaxed, simple, or modern look.

➡ **See "Installing Plank Flooring," p. 166.**

Wood-look plank tiles will enhance the beauty of any décor whether you have a contemporary, midcentury modern, rustic, traditional, artsy, or perhaps eclectic style home. >> >> >>

Wood-look plank tiles are increasingly popular and are available in a range of colors, sizes, textures, and finishes.

Some wood-look tiles have very realistic features from knots to striations (left), while others have minimal patterns and subtle colors for a more modern clean look (right).

The rich grain pattern on this wood-look tile would make a bold statement on any floor.

Wood-look tiles can create a warm rustic look on any floor without the mess of sanding and finishing that comes with real wood.

SPECIALTY TILE (CONTINUED)

Textured and graphic tiles

Architectural, sculptural, 3-D, textured, graphic, and *shaped* are all words to describe the new wave of ceramic and porcelain tiles that fall outside the old prevailing view that tile should be flat and square. Instead of creating a tile wall that becomes a simple backdrop, these tiles often are the outstanding feature on a wall and everything else may become background noise.

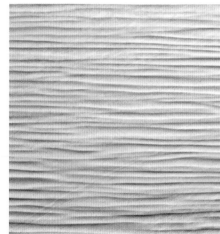 

When used on a wall, textured tiles create a beautiful dimensional surface, especially when combined with overhead lighting. The detail photo at right highlights the tile's 3-D effect.

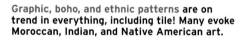

Graphic, boho, and ethnic patterns are on trend in everything, including tile! Many evoke Moroccan, Indian, and Native American art.

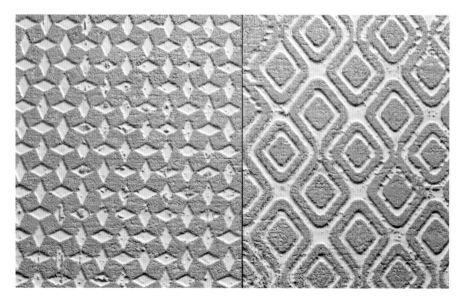

These two tiles are an interesting combination of textures and patterns and give a real architectural feel to any feature wall, whether interior or exterior.

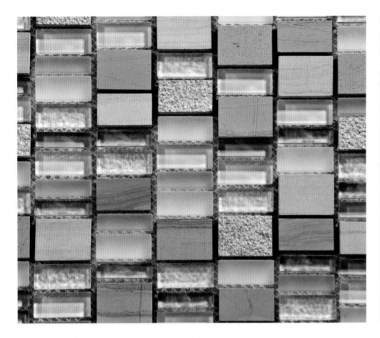

Many netted mosaics combine different types of tile for a unique installation. This one shows frosted and clear glass along with natural stone, textured, and smooth tiles.

A textured, old-world style is sometimes used to enhance that feel in a commercial setting or to blend new and old in a more artistic home environment.

Pickets and hexagons in the ever-popular neutral gray can be combined to create one-of-a-kind patterns limited only by your imagination.

This single tile combines cuts from multiple varied stones and would add a lot of texture and interest to any installation.

TRIM

Every tile installation (except for the simplest floor) requires some amount of trim to finish edges and make smooth transitions between surfaces: between a counter and a backsplash or butcher-block cutting board or between a tub surround and wall. Trim tiles come in different types, each shape designed to create a different kind of edge, corner, or transition between surfaces. Here is a rundown of the most popular types of trim.

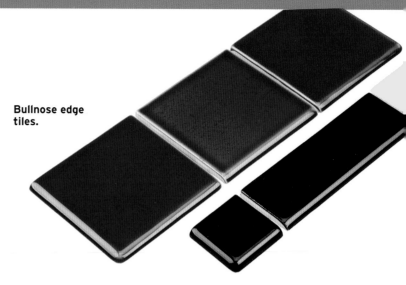

Bullnose edge tiles.

Surface bullnose

Square surface bullnose tiles have rounded and glazed edges and are used at the perimeter of a tiled surface (counter, backsplash) to create a clean finished edge. They can also be used where two tiled walls meet to make a clean outside corner. The long edges on narrow surface bullnose tiles (see the top photo at right) are rounded, making them useful for finishing the edges on thick tile countertops.

Quarter-round

Quarter-rounds are another type of edge trim used to produce a finished outside edge for a field-tiled surface, say a shower enclosure or kitchen backsplash. Quarter-rounds with a single rounded end are called "beaks" and are used to trim outside corners. Because of their shape, quarter-rounds can be used to compensate for the thickness of the substrate (backerboard, mud mortar bed). For example, when trimming around an undermount sink, one edge of each quarter-round butts up to the surface tiles, while the other edge rests on the top of the sink flange.

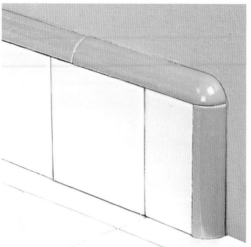 

Quarter-round as a trim **for a simple backsplash.**   Quarter-round trim **around an undermount sink.**

Cove

Often used in older tiled bathrooms, cove trim is used to create a concave rounded corner between a floor and a wall or between two adjacent walls. Cove corners are easier to keep clean than square corners, especially in high-use areas, like around kitchen sinks. Unfortunately, cove trim isn't very popular today, so it's not readily available.

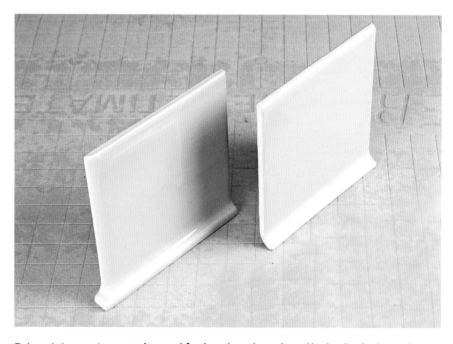

Retro-style cove base **can be used for baseboard or where the backsplash meets the countertop.**

V-cap and radius bullnose

A traditional front edge trim for bathroom vanities and kitchen countertops, V-cap trim can also be used to create a classy looking finished edge around any counter surface. V-cap is practical because its raised, curved top edge prevents round objects (such as eggs–hence, its nickname "egg saver") and spilled liquids from rolling and dripping off the countertop.

Radius bullnose trim has a deep curved edge. It was originally used to trim counters, showers, and other surfaces that were laid on top of a mud bed. Like quarter-round, it can be used to make up for the thickness of substrates.

Liners and listellos

Liners and listellos are long, narrow pieces of tile often used between courses of field tiles as decorative accents. Liner tiles may be made of glass, ceramic, or natural stone and have flat, rope-shape, or rounded surfaces. Listellos are similar to liners but are more decorative. Their surfaces are typically adorned with relief patterns or hand-painted designs. Listellos can be used between or around field tiles or next to edge trim to add unique detailing.

Tile base

Manufactured with a bullnose edge, tile base can be used around a floor in lieu of wood baseboard trim. The beauty of a tile base is that it cleans with ease, never needs painting, and doesn't get dinged or dented. If tile base isn't available to match your selected tile, cut your own out of the field tile, placing the cut edge down, next to the floor.

V-cap and radius bullnose.

Egg-saver V-cap has a raised edge.

Liners are available in a variety of shapes and colors.

Floor tiles often have companion base tiles.

A tile base can be functional and attractive.

COLOR

Complement or contrast

Choosing the color of your tile is one of the most basic and important decisions you can make. People often start their tile selection process by simply picking a color they like. But beyond personal preferences, the right color for your installation should suit your lifestyle and be practical to live with.

Bold colors and decorative patterns can add visual punch to a bathroom to help kick-start your mornings. However, soft, muted colors can lend a soothing look to help calm everyday tensions. If you entertain often, choosing bold colors or patterned tiles for your powder room can provide an enjoyable surprise for your guests. Children's bathrooms can also benefit from a colorful palette; just make sure your choice will stand the test of time as kids mature into teenagers (stay away from borders of toy boats or castles). Instead of picking tile that matches the color of the walls or specific furnishings, choose tile colors that complement the room's overall palette and mood.

The earthy stone tiles of this fireplace surround contrast with the bright wall color while harmonizing with the upholstered furnishings.

Borders can outline or delineate the field tile with a design, color, shape, or decorative element.

For a Zen-like restful retreat, choose soothing colors and natural textures, like stone and river rock.

The mosaic border and large light-colored tile give this room the feel of a classic Roman house.

Terra-cotta pavers are wonderfully versatile, equally at home among elegant furnishings and rustic surroundings.

Express your style

It is not surprising that some types of tile suit a particular home's decor better than others. For example, terra-cotta pavers that would look out of place in a postmodern interior are a natural choice for a Spanish or Southwest-style home. Similarly, ultramodern glass or metal tiles may clash with Victorian, colonial, and other traditional styles. Installing tile that runs against the grain of your home's decor can add an unexpected fashion-forward look to an otherwise plain and pre-dictable interior; just make sure you won't regret your boldness after living with the tile for a year or two or when the time comes to sell your home.

ASK FOR DESIGN HELP

It's one thing to choose tile as a finished material, say blue ceramic tile with iridescent glass trim, and another to create an overall tile design that looks good and suits both your lifestyle and your home's decor. Unless you have experience at this, coming up with a well-conceived tile design can be a little intimidating. Fortunately, most tile stores have design-ers on staff that can help you develop a good plan for your installation. Start by looking through current how-to books and home magazines and websites to get some ideas of how tile is incorporated into different settings. Make photocopies of images or bookmark websites that speak to your taste.

TILE SHAPE AND ORIENTATION

Make patterns

The shape and orientation of field tiles have a strong affect on the overall look of any tile installation. Square tiles can be laid with their edges running parallel or diagonal to walls and counters. Rectangular tiles are commonly laid in a "brick" pattern, with tiles staggered in alternating rows. Octagonal and hexagonal tiles can be oriented in either of two ways, each with a slightly different look.

While it's more expensive and time-consuming to lay tile diagonally, it's usually more visually interesting and, when laid on a large surface like a floor or wall, can make a room look bigger than it really is. Diagonally laid tiles can provide a good visual transition between tile and an existing floor. Combining different tile shapes within the same layout can also perk up the look.

Setting tile diagonally can often make an area look larger and more interesting.

You can enliven a gorgeous granite slab countertop with a riveting, diamond backsplash. The light grout color is not a problem in this high-use kitchen because it is used on the wall.

Laying your tile in a straight pattern is the easiest and most common orientatic

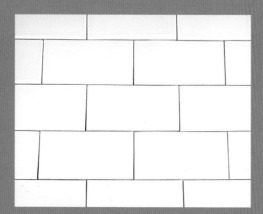

Brick or subway patterns of tile are very popular and make a great retro look.

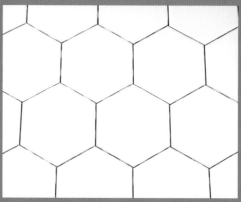

When setting hex tiles, look at both orientations to choose your favorite. This pattern gives a staggered look when viewed from this angle.

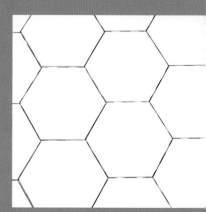

This alternate view may be more interesting or less busy in one tiled area or another.

Combining tile with other materials

There's no rule that says you have to use the same kind of tile throughout an entire installation. Using different kinds of tile together can be a good idea, both in terms of design and of economy. For example, setting a few expensive decorative tiles in a field of cheaper ceramic field tiles can add panache to your installation, while allowing you to stay within a budget. In an entryway, try adding some decorative tiles to highlight the risers on stairs sporting more-affordable terra-cotta treads.

Also consider that not every surface in your kitchen or bathroom need be covered with tile. A current trend is to avoid using tile in places where cleaning grout is an issue. That's why many of our clients choose to install solid granite or wooden butcher-block countertops and reserve tile for the backsplashes. This arrangement provides a practical, easy-to-clean-and-maintain working surface, while preserving the attractive visual impact of colorful tile. Other possibilities are using tile on kitchen countertops and covering the floor with cork or linoleum.

More expensive, handmade decorative tiles are featured in this installation along with less costly, equally beautiful stone field tiles.

Decorative tiles on the stair risers help create a dramatic and welcoming entrance.

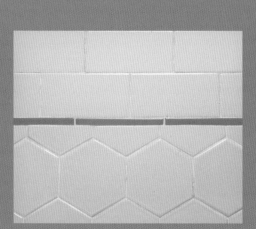

A combination of different tile shapes and colors can make your design more intriguing.

Add some small decos, set in the opposition axis, for unique pattern.

Slab counters don't always need a manufactured edge. Adhere your favorite complimentary edge tiles to the front of the flat edge on a granite or marble slab for a unique look.

GROUT COLOR AND JOINT SIZE

Grout should complement the color of the tile and harmonize with any color variations or contrasts in decos.

Complement the tile

The color and size of the grout joints between your tiles significantly affect the look of the overall tile installation. In most applications, it's appropriate to choose a grout color that complements the tile color, such as almond-colored grout with light tan tile. Complementary grout is also a good choice when you don't want the grout lines to detract from patterned or decorative tiles.

Alternatively, you can create a striking effect by choosing grout that contrasts with the color of the tile. The greater the color difference or contrast between the grout and the tile, the more dramatic the effect. You can use two (or more) different colors of grout in the same tile installation, but the colors can bleed into one another unless you mask off one area, apply the first color grout, then let it dry before applying the other color.

Grout joint size also affects the look of your tile job. With most kinds of tile, spacers (ranging in size from $1/16$ in. to $1/2$ in. and up) are used to create open joints between the tiles for the grout.

Generally, the larger the grout joint, the more rustic the look of the installation. When laying irregular stone or terra-cotta pavers, wider grout joints deemphasize the size differences between tiles and make it easier to lay them. Narrower grout joints tend to create a more elegant, refined appearance, especially with mosaic and decorative tile layouts. Narrow joints are also easier to keep clean in a bathroom or high-use area and are usually used for polished natural stone.

DEALING WITH SIZE VARIATIONS

If there's a size variation of more than $1/16$ in. between tiles or if you're setting tile on a floor that's not perfectly flat, use a grout joint no narrower than $3/16$ in. or $1/4$ in. Wider grout joints allow for more variation, and the tiles are much easier to set with the additional space between them.

White grout stands out from this gray limestone and brightens the installation.

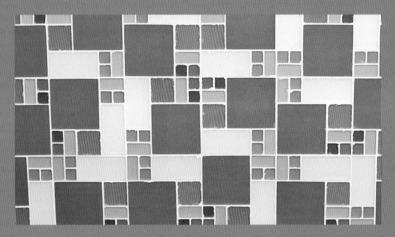

Narrow grout joints help keep the look of a mural design intact. They also work well with tiles of the same size for a clean, modern, elegant, or more refined look.

Gray grout acts in concert with the gray limestone to show off the stone's natural variation and beauty.

Whoa! Red grout can be striking in a commercial installation such as a restaurant, or for art projects. It's a little strong for most homes, unless red is your signature color.

Narrow joints and light grout are usually used with white or light ceramic tile.

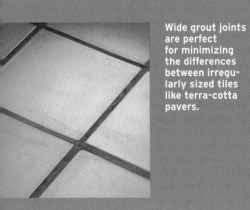

Wide grout joints are perfect for minimizing the differences between irregularly sized tiles like terra-cotta pavers.

The joints in natural stone floors are usually very narrow.

PRACTICAL CONSIDERATIONS

Whether you're improving a bathroom vanity, refurbishing a kitchen counter, or installing a new floor, there are many things to consider beyond tile's physical attributes when choosing the right tile for your project. Some of these practical issues are pretty obvious: Is the tile good looking, affordable, and durable? Other factors are less apparent: Is the tile too slippery for the chosen location? Does the tile show dirt readily and is it difficult to maintain? Are the necessary types of trim available? Overlooking any of these concerns can, at best, make your tile project more frustrating. At worst, you might end up with tile that doesn't match your needs and lifestyle.

Durability

Who wants to go to all the expense and trouble of installing tile that ends up looking worn and damaged in a year or two? Try to match the durability characteristics of tile with the demands of the surface it's used on. For example, it's foolish to install tile with low wear resistance, like a standard ceramic or a soft stone like marble, in a high-use kitchen where heavy pots and pans are used often. In this situation, durable porcelain or hard granite tile is a much better choice. But that doesn't mean that softer tiles aren't a good choice for other installations, including bathroom floors, tub enclosures, and vanity tops.

Safety

As beautiful as tile is, it isn't the safest choice for every application. Avoid using tiles with a high-gloss glaze or high-polished surface on floors. To prevent people from slipping in entryways, bathrooms, kitchens, and other areas likely to get wet, choose a tile with a matte finish or a textured surface. Tiles are rated for their slip resistance, under both wet and dry conditions. If you're concerned about family members or guests (especially children and the elderly) slipping and falling, be sure to check these ratings at your dealer before buying floor tiles.

TRADE SECRET

If you're saving money by buying bargain closeouts or discontinued tile, make sure to buy enough not only for the job but also for any future tile expansions or repairs. Don't get caught short!

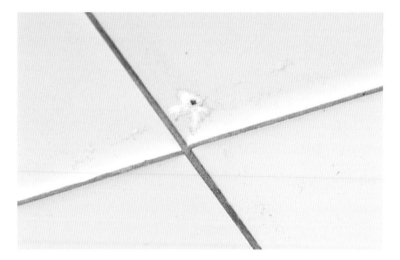

Wear and tear **on soft tile can be visible in just a short time. Match the tile durability to its usage.**

Porcelain tile provides **a durable, beautiful entry.**

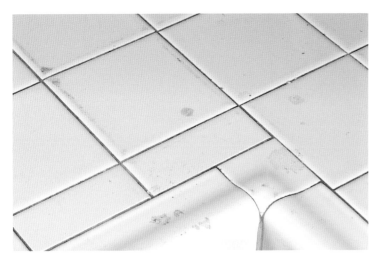

Light colored tiles **tend to show every bit of dirt or coffee drips.**

Even after being sealed, **light colored grout will stain if the spill isn't mopped or cleaned up immediately.**

Maintenance

If cleaning tile isn't your idea of a good time, there are some tile and grout choices that you should avoid. While it's generally durable, stone tile requires more upkeep than other kinds of tile, including periodic resealing. On the plus side, the patterns and shade variations of natural and faux stone tiles tend to hide dirt and pet fur. Likewise, you'll spend more time cleaning porous stain-prone tiles, such as marble and limestone, making them a bad choice for kitchen counters where food and liquids are spilled on a daily basis.

Color choice also affects how often tile needs cleaning. White ceramic and light marble tiles look terrific when they're new; but unless they're kept spotlessly clean, they'll show every bit of dirt and grime. Earth tone or medium gray tiles are much easier to live with and a much better candidate for high-use surfaces, like counters and floors. Shiny, dark-colored tiles tend to show water spots, making them a poor choice for a kitchen backsplash or shower enclosure. Grout color has an impact on tile maintenance as well. White grout used on tiled kitchen or bar countertops quickly show stains and grime, unless you diligently clean up spills promptly. Gray and earth-tone grout colors don't reveal stains as readily, and help conceal dirt that accumulates in the wide grout joints of a tiled floor. >> >> >>

Tile isn't always the right choice Tile's great looks and typically long-lasting, easy-to-maintain qualities are what lead most people to install it in their homes. But tile isn't a good choice for every application. For instance, a dropped glass will break on a tile floor but it may bounce on a linoleum or cork floor. Children and the elderly may slip and fall on tile floors, and pet claws may scratch up softer stone tiles. Some effects can be mitigated by the use of plastic mats on countertops and area rugs on floors, but usually it's better to choose another material for your installation.

PRACTICAL CONSIDERATIONS (CONTINUED)

Cost and availability

As we like to tell our clients, even Bill Gates has a budget. When you go into a tile store, tell the salespeople how much you have to spend, so they can steer you toward the kinds of tile you can afford. Once you've picked your tile, make sure to check the price of the matching trim. Field tiles can be very inexpensive, but their associated trim (V-cap, surface bullnose) can cost far more. (We once did a countertop with a moderately priced field tile that had matching end caps costing more than $20 apiece!)

Is the tile you've picked in stock at the tile store, or does it have to be special ordered or custom made? It's prudent to order 20% more special-order tile than you'll need, because of potential delays and the possibility that if you reorder, the new tile may not match what you have. Once you've picked the field tile you like, check to see which trim pieces are available. Standard ceramic and other popular tiles have a wide range of available trim; yet, for many other kinds of tile, there's little choice in trim or no trim at all. If you can't get the matching trim you desire, consider substituting other kinds of tile. For example, instead of matching quarter-rounds or bullnose trim, substitute a rope liner (or similar decorative border tile) to finish the edge of a back-splash or wainscoting.

Even if you can get matching trim, the lengths of most trim pieces don't match the dimensions of the field tiles, which really disturbs some people. Also check to see how consistently the trim matches the color, texture, and/or pattern of the field tile.

How much tile to buy

Once you've decided on the kinds of tile to use for your installation, you'll need to calculate how much to buy. Field tile is ordered by the square foot, and trim pieces are ordered by the piece or linear foot. For most basic tile jobs using standard ceramic or porcelain tile, we recommend ordering 10% to 20% more tile than you actually need. This compensates for breakage, miscut tiles, and future repairs, should tiles get damaged. (Some tile and home supply stores allow culled tiles to be returned; check their policies before making your purchase.) Because they're more apt to break, you should order 25% more for fragile tiles like glass and onyx. If you're working

Trim pieces may not be the same size as field tile. If this bothers your aesthetic sense, check with the tile store to confirm that everything will match in size.

A caution with stone-look tiles: The trim may not match exactly. In this case, the bullnose is missing texture and pattern along its edge.

Wax pencils in contrasting colors are great for marking chips or defects as you sort and mix your tiles.

Rectified Tiles

Rectified tiles are ceramic or porcelain tiles that have been mechanically processed to ensure that all the tiles are uniform in length and width, allowing tiles to be set closer to one another for narrower grout joints. This provides a clean modern look to your tile installation, and a reputable tile store will be able to assist you in choosing from their rectified tiles. Because of the extra processing, these tiles tend to be a little more expensive.

Another thing to be aware of is that many rectified tiles have very square edges. While this makes for a highly consistent grout joint, it also means that you need to be extra careful when handling any rectified tile. A slight bump against another tile or a tool may result in a chip along the edge. When using rectified tile for plane changes, as on steps or an outside corner, consider using bullnose tile (if available) or metal trim edges (like Schluter®).

Even with rectified tiles, height (of adjacent tile edges placed next to one another) and warpage can still vary slightly from tile to tile, which creates "lippage," otherwise known to most of us as a "toe-tripper" on a floor. This is why a flat substrate is still your first step in creating a floor or wall surface that has minimal lippage.

with stone or other natural tiles, you might need up to 50% more to allow you to match veining and grain patterns across a surface. Tile layout also affects how much to buy: You'll need about 15% more tile for any given diagonal layout than for a straight layout. Don't forget to order extra trim tiles too: about 20% more. For counters, add two additional corner pieces to the number you need as corners often don't accurately match the size and profile of other trim. After you bring the tiles home, examine them and mark any damaged areas with a wax pencil. Set those tiles aside for cut pieces.

PERSONAL SAFETY GEAR

A FEW INEXPENSIVE
SAFETY ACCESSORIES
PROTECT YOUR EYES,
EARS, LUNGS, AND
HANDS.

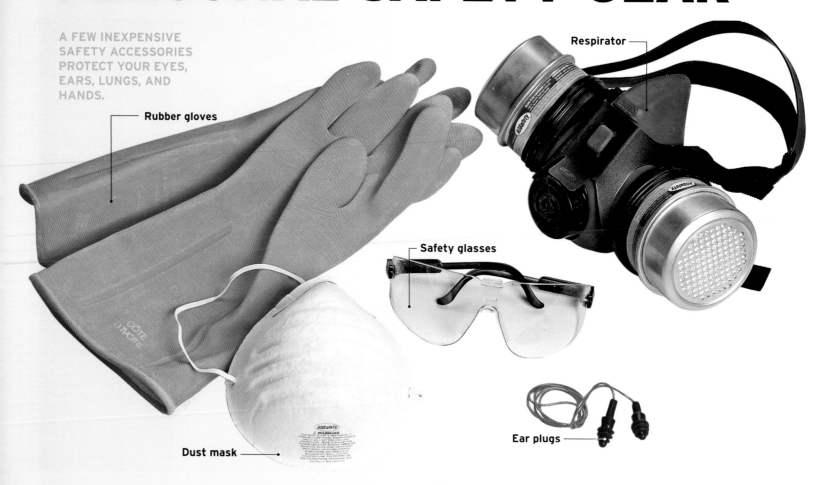

Rubber gloves

Respirator

Safety glasses

Dust mask

Ear plugs

There's no good reason not to guard your eyes, ears, lungs, hands, and knees from the hazards and rigors of tile demolition, preparation, and installation by wearing the proper safety gear.

Safety goggles or glasses

Whether you're operating power tools or trimming with tile nippers, you must wear safety glasses or goggles to protect your eyes from chips, splinters, and other flying debris. Vented goggles can be worn over regular eyeglasses.

Ear protection

Whether you choose in-ear style plugs or over-ear protectors, it's important to always wear ear protection when using power tools or cutting on the wet saw. The noise gener-

Dressed for success. Always use eye protection when breaking up tile and hearing protection when using power tools. Wear gloves to protect hands from sharp edges.

ated during cutting, grinding, and drilling is often loud enough to cause damage to your sense of hearing, even after only brief exposure.

Masks and respirators

Two-strap disposable dust masks help protect your lungs from dust caused by grouts and thinsets that contain silica. For protection from more-hazardous dusts and fumes that occur when grinding floors or spreading membranes, wear a half-mask cartridge filter respirator. These feature removable cartridges that may be changed to suit the job at hand (check the manufacturer's recommendations). A much more costly but incomparably effective alternative is a powered air-purifying respirator (PAPR). This apparatus features a full face mask that's supplied with clean air pumped through a flexible hose from a battery-powered belt pack with a fan and filter cartridges. PAPRs are the only kind of mask that provides safe protection for bearded users working with hazardous materials, such as particulates or organic vapors (regular masks don't seal fully against a bearded face).

Gloves

There are two kinds of gloves useful for tile prep, installation, repair, and maintenance: Work gloves are great for protecting your hands when handling sharp-edged materials or during demolition operations. Rubber gloves protect your skin from dryness and irritation during tile grouting and sealing as well as when performing routine cleaning.

Knee pads

Although not strictly safety gear, knee pads are a must for reducing the risk of knee injuries or problems incurred during all phases of work on a tile floor. Whether you choose a single pad to kneel on or a pair of knee pads to wear, test several before you buy and choose the model you find most comfortable.

Mixing thinset and grout **can generate fine dust that can injure your lungs. Wear a dust mask.**

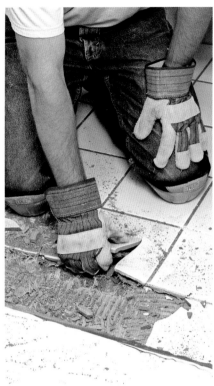

A sturdy pair of work gloves **keep hands from getting torn up during demolition.**

A powered air-purifying respirator **provides protection against many toxic fumes and dusts.**

Knee pads come as either single **pads or pairs of wearable protectors.**

DEMOLITION TOOLS

DEMOLITION TOOLS HELP TACKLE THE FIRST
PHASE OF A TILE JOB: REMOVING OLD COUNTERS,
BACKSPLASHES, OR FLOORS.

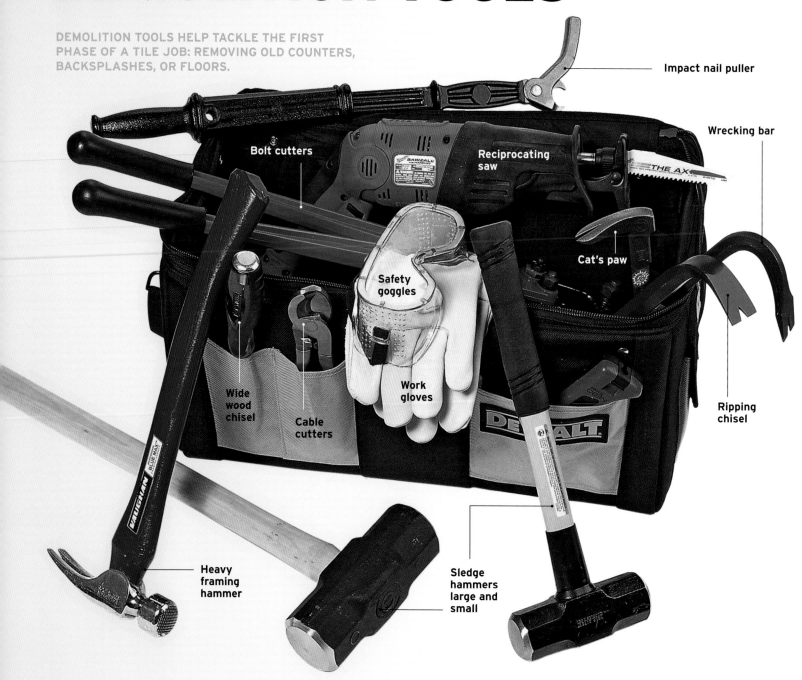

Impact nail puller

Wrecking bar

Bolt cutters

Reciprocating saw

Cat's paw

Safety goggles

Work gloves

Ripping chisel

Wide wood chisel

Cable cutters

Heavy framing hammer

Sledge hammers large and small

Depending on what you plan to remove or tear apart, you'll need a complement of hand and power tools. In addition to the tools described here, you'll also need a utility knife (with retractable blade and lots of extra blades), screwdrivers, adjustable slip-joint pliers, 16-ounce claw hammer, a hacksaw (with a fine-toothed blade), a wet/dry shop vacuum,

a broom and dustpan (for cleanup chores), and extension cords for power equipment.

Chisels and prybars

Special chisels designed for tile work have a very hard carbide tip welded at the end of their shaft. The carbide tip resists dulling when working with any kind of tile.

Struck by a regular hammer, a carbide chisel is useful for removing dried thinset from a floor, knocking tiles off a backsplash during demolition, and removing tile for small repairs.

Flat or broad-bladed prybars are ideal for lifting up old tack strip and flooring, pulling apart old countertops, and doing

CHISELS AND PRYBARS

The hardened tip of a carbide chisel helps break up tiles and separate them from their thinset bed.

Use a prybar in conjunction with a hammer to remove old tile.

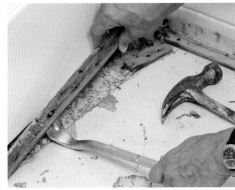

A prybar is used here to pull up carpet tack strips and remove nails and staples.

most of the heavy lifting you need during demo. The nail claw on the prybar or a cat's paw is very handy for pulling out old nails and staples.

Floor scraper

Before you tile over concrete, you must do a thorough job of removing old flooring, glue, and paint to prepare the surface properly for tile. Floor scrapers are perfect for the task. Long-handled scrapers are useful for removing vinyl over concrete, but the short ones (called wall scrapers) give you better leverage when you have a tough area to strip or scrape. With either one, get lots of extra blades as you will go through them fast.

Reciprocating saw

A reciprocating saw has a motor-driven blade that moves back and forth like a handsaw, only much faster. This saw makes short work of cutting apart cabinets, cutting out bad sections in subflooring, and so on. When fitted with a metal-cutting blade, it will cut through plumbing and frozen bolts; with a special attachment called a Grout Grabber® (available from www.groutgrabber.com), it'll even remove old grout.

>> >> >>

The sharp, wide edge of a floor scraper digs under vinyl flooring, removing it quickly.

Versatile and powerful, a reciprocating saw accepts blades for cutting wood or metal, as well as special accessories like this one for sawing through grout.

DEMOLITION TOOLS (CONTINUED)

Rotary hammer

An electric rotary hammer is similar to a jackhammer, just smaller, lighter, and better suited to DIY work. The reciprocal action of its replaceable chisel makes short work of chipping away high spots on concrete and removing thinset, tile, and stone from an old floor or countertop during demolition. While you might wish to purchase one for a large project, they're readily available at most rental places.

A rotary hammer is powerful enough to chip through stone tiles to remove an old floor.

TRADE SECRET

When scraping glue and flooring residue that are particularly difficult to remove, use a heat gun (like a blow dryer, but much hotter) to soften the old adhesives or vinyl before scraping.

PREPARATION AND REPAIR TOOLS

Scoring backerboard with this tool allows you to snap it to size, just like a pane of glass.

Getting any surface ready for tile installation calls for a mix of both hand and power tools, as described in this section. You'll also need a putty knife or two (wide and narrow), a paint roller and cover, a circular saw and a jigsaw (for cutting countertop rough tops), a utility knife, a hammer, a notched trowel, and a level.

Backerboard scoring tool

A scoring tool is indispensable for cutting backerboard to size to use under backsplashes, countertops, and (sometimes) floors. This specialized tool's carbide tip scores a line into concrete backerboard, allowing you to snap it along the line, just like glass.

Angle grinder

A 4-in. or 5-in. angle grinder performs any number of useful tasks for surface preparation and tile installation. Fitted with a diamond or carbide blade, it's handy for making sink cutouts in backerboard or slicing damaged tiles into pieces for easy removal. An angle grinder fitted with a cup wheel is good for cleaning up small areas of concrete in lieu of a concrete grinder.

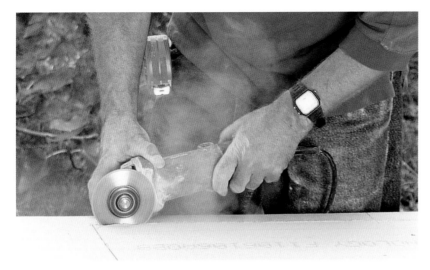

An angle grinder can be fitted with a variety of accessories. Although it kicks up clouds of dust when fitted with a masonry blade, it cuts through tile and backerboard with ease.

Concrete grinder

For cleaning up the surface of large concrete floors, you'll need a concrete grinder. It has a carbide/diamond cup wheel that's effective for grinding off high spots on a large concrete slab or removing glue and foreign substances that will interfere with tile bonding. Hooked up to a vacuum, these grinders (available at rental yards) are almost dustless.

Electric drill and accessories

A portable or corded electric drill, preferably a variable-speed model, makes short work of driving screws into your backerboard during surface preparation. A drill is also perfect for powering a paddle-wheel mixer to blend thinset for bonding backerboard and tile. Because of the heavy nature of tile materials, a corded model is preferable for mixing as it has the necessary torque and no battery to run down.

➡ See "Mixing Thinset," p. 81

Grout saw

The grout saw, a little hand tool, has a carbide/diamond edge. By scraping back and forth along a grout joint, you can remove grout before doing a repair or replacement.

⚠ **WARNING**
A first-aid kit, complete with eyewash, is a good thing to have on hand before you start any project and especially if you're unfamiliar or inexperienced with the particular hazards that different tools and materials present.

An electric concrete grinder quickly abrades high spots and removes stuck-on residue from a slab floor.

The delicate job of removing grout is best left to the narrow carbide-impregnated blade of a grout saw.

TILE-CUTTING TOOLS

ALTHOUGH IT'S EXPENSIVE AND A BIT
MESSY, AN ELECTRIC WATER SAW CAN
MAKE ALL YOUR TILE-CUTTING CHORES
MUCH EASIER.

There are many ways of cutting or drilling tile, each using a different tool. Tile nippers, cutting boards, and electric-powered water saws make straight, angled, and curved cuts. An electric drill fitted with a carbide-tipped bit cleanly bores holes through tile for pipes and wires. Each tool has its pros and cons, and your choice depends on the type of tile you're cutting and the kinds of cuts you need to make. Whichever tool you use, always wear eye protection when cutting tile because chips and shards can fly far and fast and do considerable damage.

Tile nippers

Tile nippers (or tile biters) work like pliers with carbide-tipped jaws. They cut tile by nibbling it away, one little piece at a time; you close the jaws on the tile while applying a downward twisting motion. They're especially handy for curved and L- or U-shaped cuts; but with some practice, you can do just about any cut. Some nippers use a compound leverage system, which makes cutting porcelain and other hard tiles easier.

Water saws

For most tile jobs, biters and a cutting board are more than adequate. But when making miters and inside cuts or working with stone or glass tiles, only a water, or wet, saw will do. These motorized saws have a narrow diamond-impregnated blade that grinds its way through the tile. The tile is held on top of a sliding table and moved past the stationary blade during a cut. Water supplied by a small submerged pump flushes out debris and keeps the blade running cool. A sealed pan under the table and motor acts as a water reservoir. Water saws are messy to use but they leave cleaner, smoother cut edges than any other type of cutter.

Water saws may be rented at your local rental store or purchased at a home supply store. The saw comes with a blade for cutting standard ceramic tile; you'll have to buy special blades for cutting glass and harder materials like granite. Take a sample of the tile you'll be cutting to make sure the saw's sliding tray is large enough to accommodate it.

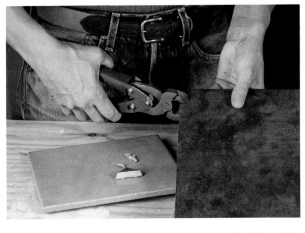

Trimming even the hardest tiles **is an almost effortless task with these newer compound nippers.**

Quick and quiet to use, **a cutting board is an affordable tool for straight cuts in a variety of types of tile.**

Cutting board

Quick and quiet to use, cutting boards are marvelous tools for trimming tile to size. Cutting boards use a carbide wheel that slides over the tile and scores the surface. The tools' breaker bar then snaps the tile in two along the score line. Cutting boards come in a variety of sizes, from compact to huge. Purchase the board that'll handle the largest tile cuts you need to make.

Rubbing stone

Cut tile edges are sharp and hazardous (they'll cut you like a knife) as well as unsightly, compared to factory tile edges. Therefore, it's advisable to smooth the edges of cut tiles with a rubbing stone. Hold the stone at a 45° angle to the face of the tile and rub parallel to the cut edge. This rounds over the edge slightly and even blends out small chips in the glaze.

Hole saw

Some bathroom, laundry room, and kitchen installations may require holes for plumbing fixtures and pipes. The easiest way to bore these is with a hole saw chucked in an electric drill. Relton Corporation makes long-lasting hole saws that bore through the hardest of tiles (available at: http://www.mytoolstore.com/relton/tubsaw.html). Buy a saw that's slightly larger in diameter than the hole you need to bore.

A rubbing stone **can smooth stone edges or sand the sharp edge of a cut tile.**

Specifically made for boring **through tile, a hole saw drills out a tile for plumbing fixtures and pipes.**

MARKING STRAIGHT CUTS

We mark the cuts for tiles that go against walls at the edge of a counter or floor by transferring the distance directly from the counter or floor to the tile. This ensures that the cut piece will fit, even if the wall isn't parallel to the tile. You may find the method a bit confusing at first because the tile's orientation is reversed during the marking process. To help you keep track of the tile's orientation during marking and cutting, start by drawing an arrow on the "good" portion of the tile so that it points toward the "waste" portion that will be cut off ❶.

Now mark one edge of the tile to be cut (the workpiece) by setting it between the wall and the last full field tile, with the arrow pointing away from wall ❷. Here it points away from the wall but after cutting, you will flip the tile and it will point to the wall. Be sure to use a spacer between the workpiece and the wall, so you'll have space for a caulk joint. To account for the caulk joint, mark the workpiece at the edge of the field tile's spacer ❸. Now slide the workpiece over to other side of the field tile and mark the other edge at the spacer as before ❹. Connect the two marks with a pencil and you're ready to cut the tile. Remember, when the tile is set in place, the cut edge will go toward the wall (the direction in which the arrow should point) ❺. Be sure to use a rubbing stone to smooth the edges.

Use a wax pencil to mark your cut lines on glazed tiles when accuracy is not an issue.

1 Drawing an arrow on the tile will help you remember its orientation.

2 Place a spacer against the wall to allow for the grout joint.

3 Make a pencil mark on the side of the spacer where the cut tile will be set.

4 Move the tile to the opposite end of the space and mark the other side of the cut.

5 Dry-fit the tile before you apply thinset, and it should be perfect.

MARKING DIAGONAL CUTS

1 Tape adjacent edges of the tile before you make marks for diagonal cuts.

2 Place a spacer against the wall to allow for grout and align the tile edge parallel with the set tile next to it.

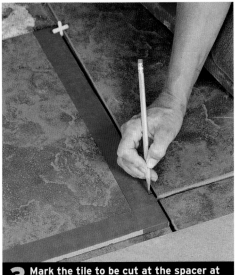

3 Mark the tile to be cut at the spacer at the intersection of the tiles.

4 Move the tile (same orientation) to the adjacent grout joint and mark it.

5 Use a scrap of tile or small level to connect your pencil marks.

When square tiles are set diagonally, instead of parallel to the wall surfaces, you'll have to trim the tiles around the edges of your installation. The process is roughly the same as marking straight cuts (see the facing page), except that the adjacent sides of the workpiece are marked, instead of the opposite sides.

If the tile you're working with is hard to mark with a pencil, apply masking tape along the edges **1**. Set one spacer against the wall (to create room for a caulk joint) and another against the field tile that's already been set, to help you keep the workpiece parallel to the set tiles **2**. Make a mark on the wall-facing side of the set tile's grout line **3**. Now move the tile and both spacers to the opposite set tile and mark the other side of the cut **4**. Draw a line to connect the two marks **5**. Cut along the line, and you'll have a perfectly cut tile, ready to set.

MARKING COMPLEX CUTS

An easy and time-saving method for marking a complex shape—concave curve or irregular edge—on a tile to be cut requires the use of a paper pattern. For example, to mark a cut on a tile that butts up to a curved wall, start by cutting a piece of rosin or brown paper the size of your tile. For such a cut, a paper template will save you lots of hair pulling. Place the paper where the tile will go when set, positioning it carefully with tile spacers ❶. Now press the paper down to create a curved crease where the paper meets the wall ❷. Cut the paper along the creased line with scissors, then put the paper back in place ❸. Use a pencil to draw a line parallel to the curved wall, holding the pencil flat to the baseboard molding ❹. This will create a space for grout or caulking between the tile and the wall. Cut the paper along this line, then transfer the curve to the surface of the tile ❺.

1 Start the template by laying a tile on a large piece of paper, and position with tile spacers.

2 After placing the paper template against the spacers, use your fingers to create a crease along the curved edge.

3 Use a pair of scissors to cut the template along the crease.

4 Lay the template back in place. Hold a pencil flat against the molding to allow for grout or caulk joint.

5 Place the template on the tile and transfer the curve.

CUTTING WITH TILE NIPPERS

Tile nippers or biters are simple, inexpensive hand tools useful for many tile-cutting jobs, and you can keep them handy in your pocket. However, using a nipper does require hand strength and some practice to get smooth and accurate cuts. While you can make practically any cut with a nipper, they're most practical when you need to nibble away a corner or small section of a tile.

They're also great for refining the shape of curves and complex cuts. To cut with nippers, firmly grab the tile with the tool's jaws, then apply a downward snapping motion to break off small pieces of tile, working toward your line of cut. Nippers work well on softer tile and stone, but there are special models designed to cut some glass ❶. These work by scoring and snapping the tile similar to the way you'd score and snap a pane of glass to cut it to size ❷.

A tile nipper **has large handles for leverage and sharp tips to bite into tile. Better models have carbide tips.**

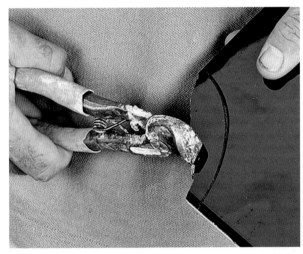

Curved cuts are easy with tile nippers, saving you trips to the saw.

CUTTING GLASS TILE

1 First use the wheel to score the tile.

2 Use the nippers to snap the tile at the score line.

THROUGH CUTS ON A WET SAW

For many simple tile jobs, a cutting board and a pair of nippers are adequate for most cuts. But some tiles, such as glass and some kinds of stone, just won't cut cleanly on a cutting board. Furthermore, there are many cuts, including curved, L-shaped, and inside cuts, that a cutting board can't handle.

For these jobs, only a powered water saw will do. Although they're messy and noisy (always wear ear protection when running a water saw), the diamond-impregnated blade cuts tiles cleaner and leaves smoother edges than you'll get from any other type of cutter. Follow the manufacturer's instructions for your particular model and always feed the tile smoothly into the blade **A**.

Some kinds of stone tile—especially slate—tend to spall (shed layers) or flake off small pieces when cut **B**. This is natural, and there's little you can do to avoid it. Save these tiles for filler pieces or use them in less visible locations.

Miter cuts

A water saw makes short work of making miter cuts at the ends of either flat tiles or shaped trim tiles, including quarter-rounds used to trim around a sink **C**, and liners used to create a frame around a tile mural **D**.

You can use your saw's miter guide to position the tile for a 45° cut, but we prefer to use a cut field tile as a jig for these cuts. To make a jig tile, mark a regular square field tile diagonally point to point **E**, and cut it in half **F**. Set this jig tile against the saw's fence and use it to position the workpiece for a miter cut **G**. When mitering quarter-rounds, do not place them flat on the saw's sliding tray. Instead, support them on edge, so they're cut in the same position in which they'll be installed **H**.

TRADE SECRET
Water is necessary to cool your tile saw's blade and wash debris away from the cut area. If the water stops, check the pump for a clogged impeller or the flow holes around the blade guard for lodged debris.

A Feed the tile smoothly through the saw.

D Some decorative tiles are mitered flat on the tray, especially if being used to frame a mirror or other element.

G First cut your piece to length, then use the tile guide to cut the miter, starting at the back edge of the tile.

B Some stone tiles, like this slate, shed layers or flake off when cut.

C Mitered quarter-rounds should have an even grout joint when they are set. These two line up perfectly.

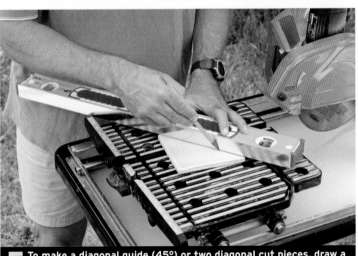
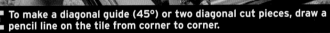

E To make a diagonal guide (45°) or two diagonal cut pieces, draw a pencil line on the tile from corner to corner.

F Line up the tile point up with the blade and cut through the tile, following your pencil mark.

H When mitering a quarter-round, you must orient the tile into the position it will lay when it is set. Do not place it flat on the saw tray.

CUTTING CURVES

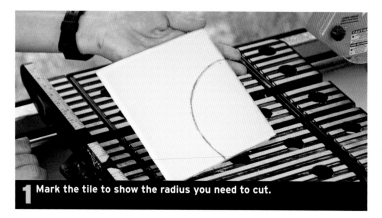

1 Mark the tile to show the radius you need to cut.

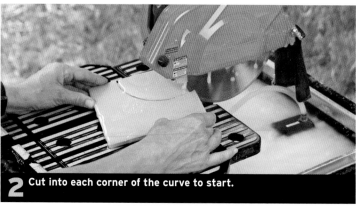

2 Cut into each corner of the curve to start.

3 Cut a number of slices into the tile, stopping at the cutting line.

4 Some slices may fall out as you cut. The more slices you cut, the easier it is to make a clean curve.

5 Tap out the slices. You'll be left with a rough edge that you'll trim with tile nippers.

6 Use the nippers to clean up the edge and smooth out the curve.

Curved cuts are usually needed around toilet flanges and other pipes. Because the cut edges of the tile are covered by either the toilet's base or an escutcheon plate, complete accuracy is not necessary. Mark the curve on the tile **1**.

First, cut into your tile at each end of the curve on the water saw **2**. Next, make a series of parallel cuts into the waste area, up to the curved line. With softer tiles, you can cut wider strips; for denser tiles, like porcelain, you'll want to make many closely spaced cuts to reduce the risk of the whole tile breaking **3**. The waste strips may fall out as you cut, which is good **4**. Once the parallel cuts are finished, use tile nippers (or a hammer) to carefully tap out the remaining waste strips from the tile **5**. Finally, use the nippers to nibble off tile up to the line of cut and clean up the rest of the curve **6**.

➤ **See "Cutting with Tile Nippers," p. 53.**

L-SHAPED CUTS

S haped cuts are often required when fitting tiles around electrical boxes on back-splashes, for example. Both L- and U-shaped cuts are easily done on a water saw.

For an L-shaped piece, first, mark out the cut on the face of the tile ❶. Continue the lines so that you can clearly see where you will be cutting ❷. Now place the tile flat on the saw and against the back stop of the saw tray. Feed the tile into the spinning blade, stopping just short of where the lines meet ❸. Carefully back out the tile. Now cut along the second line until the two cuts almost meet ❹. Lift the front edge of the tile carefully and cut all the way into first one corner, then the other until the waste piece falls out ❺.

WHAT CAN GO WRONG

When you mark the cut lines for an electrical box, leave room for the screw holes.

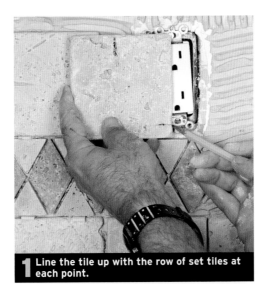

1 Line the tile up with the row of set tiles at each point.

2 Continue the vertical and horizontal cut marks from the edge of the tile.

3 Cut just to the point at which the lines intersect, not beyond.

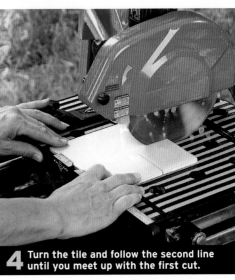

4 Turn the tile and follow the second line until you meet up with the first cut.

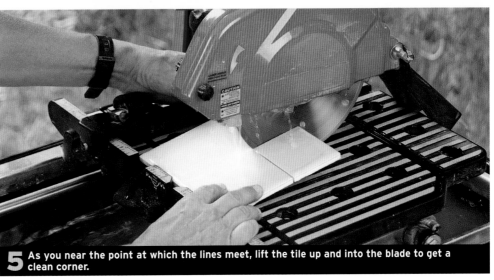

5 As you near the point at which the lines meet, lift the tile up and into the blade to get a clean corner.

U-SHAPED CUTS

U-shapes are made like L-cuts (see p. 59), except three cuts are needed. After marking out the cutting lines, cut the two parallel lines of the U ❶. Make the third cut by plunging the sawblade into the face of the tile (most saws have a knob that allows the saw head to be raised and lowered) ❷. Lower the blade slowly to make the cut, and don't cut past the two side cuts. To remove the waste to complete the shape, make a number of parallel cuts close together ❸, then break them out with tile nippers or pliers.

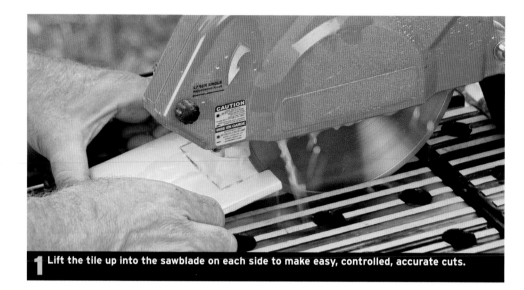

1 Lift the tile up into the sawblade on each side to make easy, controlled, accurate cuts.

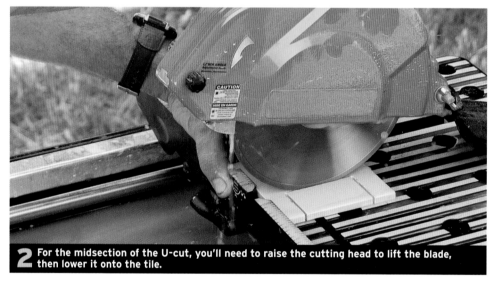

2 For the midsection of the U-cut, you'll need to raise the cutting head to lift the blade, then lower it onto the tile.

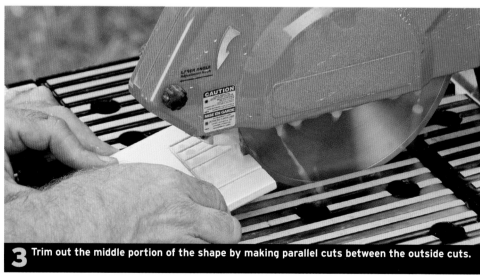

3 Trim out the middle portion of the shape by making parallel cuts between the outside cuts.

SMALL INTERNAL CUTS

Sometimes cuts need to be made in the middle of a tile, say for an electrical outlet or switch box. When a tile will completely surround an electrical outlet, the center of the tile will need to be removed by a series of plunge cuts.

On the outside surface of the tile, cover the area to be cut with blue painter's tape so that you can see your marks. Measure the distance from the edge of the tile to where the cutout should fall and mark the outline carefully. Raise the cutting head of the saw, then lower the blade onto the tile on each of the four marked lines, then plunge-cut along each line, taking care not to cut too deep into the corners ❶, ❷. If the sides of the cut area are short, and/or the tile is thick, the sawblade won't penetrate the tile. In this case, transfer your cutting lines onto the back ❸ and recut the tile, cutting slightly beyond the corners ❹. Knock the waste piece out, leaving the face with a clean cut ❺.

1 Plunge-cut to each side of the marked outline.

2 Flip the tile and cut those sides.

3 If the cut doesn't penetrate the tile, transfer the layout lines to the back.

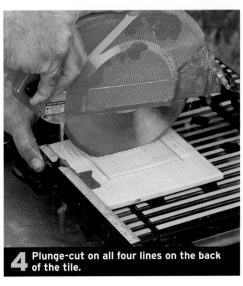

4 Plunge-cut on all four lines on the back of the tile.

5 Tap the center of the tile cut carefully until the piece pops out.

LARGE INTERNAL CUTS

To make a large internal cut for toilet flanges or large pipe, mark the circle on the back of the tile **1**. Plunge-cut four slots parallel to the edges of the upside down tile, using the edge of the circle as a guide **2**. Now cut four slots at 45° angles to the cuts you just made, extending the cuts slightly beyond where the corners meet **3**.

Turn the tile face up. You'll see your previous cut lines. Plunge the blade into each cut slot, extending the cuts until they meet at the corners **4**. Overrun the lines slightly as it will make it easier to knock out the center cut. Plunge-cut an X into the middle of the octagon **5**, then knock out the center waste by rapping it with a tile nipper **6**.

WHAT CAN GO WRONG

Don't cut too deeply or your cut marks may not be covered by the flange after installation.

1 Mark out the area to be cut as an octagon.

2 Plunge-cut along the circle, parallel to the edges of the tile. Do not cut too deep.

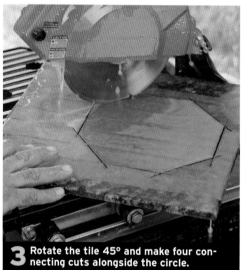

3 Rotate the tile 45° and make four connecting cuts alongside the circle.

4 Flip the tile over. Cut to each of the lines until the cuts connect.

5 Cut an X in the middle of the octagon, dividing the cutout into quarters.

6 Tap around the edges of the center cut, and the pieces will drop out.

CUTTING GLASS TILE

1 Lift the edge of the tile off the tray. Hold it in this position as you move the tray very slowly through the blade.

2 Coat the backing of the glass tile with instant glue or cyanoacrylate glue. Place a bead of glue along the cut line.

3 A quick spritz of accelerant will harden the glue and allow you to make your cut immediately.

4 The glue keeps the backing from flaking off after you make the cut.

Glass tiles require their own special blade when cut on the water saw. This blade is designed to minimize shattering and chipping of the glass and its colored backing. However, even a saw fitted with a special glass blade can chip or shatter tile. We've found that tiles shatter more often when cut laying flat on the sliding tray. You'll consistently get cleaner cuts by lifting the forward edge of the tile up off the tray **❶** and feeding it through the blade *very* slowly. If you hear the motor bog or start to slow down as you're cutting, you'll know that you are pushing the tile through too fast.

To prevent the delicate backing found on many glass tiles from flaking off, coat the backing area to be cut with cyanoacrylate glue **❷**. Apply a thin film of glue over the line of cut, then use a spray accelerant to set the glue quickly **❸**. The hardened glue prevents flaking, producing a clean-cut tile that's ready to set **❹**.

DRILLING TILE

Boring through tile to allow plumbing fixtures and pipes to pass through is an important skill you'll master quickly. All it takes is a variable-speed drill, a carbide-tipped drill bit, and a masonry hole cutter.

First, mark the center of the hole with a pencil, then place the tile on a wood scrap or other flat, rigid backing. Align the tip of the drill bit with the mark and apply a small amount of pressure while you rock the bit from side to side ❶. On most tiles, you will hear a faint cracking or scratching sound, which indicates you have scored the glaze. This dimple will prevent the bit from wandering out of position when you drill. On very soft white-bodied tiles, you can create this dimple by tapping with the corner of a carbide chisel (or a nail) .

Now bore a pilot hole with a bit that's the same diameter as the hole saw's pilot bit. Position the bit over the dimple and start the drill at a very slow speed, applying light and even pressure as you drill. As the bit penetrates the tile, it'll create a pile of dust ❷. Keep a firm grip on the tile, to prevent the bit from grabbing it and spinning it wildly. Apply some water to the hole, to lubricate the bit and keep the dust down. As water evaporates due to the heat the bit generates, keep adding it into the deepening hole. Soft white-bodied tiles usually take only a couple of minutes to drill, whereas denser tiles may take 5 minutes or even 10 minutes.

Drilling large holes

To bore a larger hole, chuck a carbide-tipped hole saw into your electric drill. Place the tile between two pieces of wood, to allow the pilot bit to go all the way through ❸. As for a small hole, apply light, even pressure as you bore, and use water as a lubricant until the bit goes all the way through the tile ❹.

1 Tap a carbide chisel to break the glaze at the center of your drill hole.

2 Drill with slow, steady pressure and a low speed.

3 Straddle the pilot-drilled tile over two pieces of wood.

4 The carbide-tipped hole saw cuts a clean round hole.

To drill softer tiles or start a repair, first tap with a hammer and carbide chisel to break the glaze. This will prevent the drill bit from wandering.

WHAT CAN GO WRONG

Never use a hammer drill to drill through tile. Its percussive force will only crack or break the tile. A glass or mirror shop will cut holes in glass tiles of any size for a small service charge.

INSTALLATION ACCESSORIES

LEVELS COME IN MANY SIZES, FROM SHORT TORPEDOES TO 8-FT. OR LONGER MODELS.

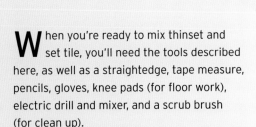

When you're ready to mix thinset and set tile, you'll need the tools described here, as well as a straightedge, tape measure, pencils, gloves, knee pads (for floor work), electric drill and mixer, and a scrub brush (for clean up).

Levels

Levels are important tools that are useful during many phases of tile work. They are handy for spotting high and low spots on floors after demolition, checking countertops for level during prep, leveling tile on counters and backsplashes, and lining up straight rows of floor tiles. They come in many sizes; you'll want one 6-in. to 12-in. torpedo level and one 3-ft. to 4-ft. basic level on hand for home tile work. Metal-bodied levels are easier to clean and will handle abuse much better than wood levels.

Bucket, sponge, and scrubber

Buckets are a mainstay tool for tile work. Use them to gather and transport your tools, collect debris from demo, mix thinset and grout, and hold water for cleanup. Plastic buckets are light, cheap, and easy to clean.

>> >> >>

Buckets, sponges, and scrubbers **are some of the most used tools for tile prep and installation.**

INSTALLATION ACCESSORIES (CONTINUED)

The 5-gal. size is great for mixing big batches and cleanup, while the $\frac{1}{2}$-gal. size is ideal for mixing small quantities of materials. Sponges are important for every aspect of tile work, and you'll need several of them for each task: cleaning, tile setting, grouting. Don't use kitchen sponges—get big yellow hydro sponges from a home center or tile store. To reduce the risk of dirt or cross-contamination from various tile procedures, use a new sponge for each task. A scrubber is a handy foam sponge with a textured side that lets you clean dry thinset or grout from tiles without scratching them.

Jambsaw

A jambsaw is a narrow saw with a medium-tooth blade that's useful for trimming off the bottoms of doorway trim, to simplify setting floor tiles around door jambs.

Beating block and mallet

After setting tiles in place, embed them into the thinset by tapping them with a hammer and rubber-coated, wooden beating block. You can also even out the surface of smaller tiles by embedding them with a beating block. A rubber-headed mallet is preferable for tapping and seating tiles 12 in. sq. or larger.

Suction-cup tool

Megasize suction-cup tools, similarly used by professionals to lift large mirrors, are also very handy for handling large tiles. The tool has a pump-actuated suction handle and is a real lifesaver for lifting big, heavy tiles like natural stone, especially when you need to lift an already-set tile to check it for thinset coverage.

 See "Tiling an Entry Area," pp. 150–152.

Use the scrubbing side of a scrubber to clean thinset from a tile surface.

Trimming the bottom of a door jamb with a jambsaw lets you easily set floor tiles around it.

A rubber-faced beating block or mallet is used to help embed tiles in thinset.

A suction-cup tool is handy for lifting and moving heavy floor tiles.

TRADE SECRET
Apply a self-sticking plastic cover over the vials of your level to protect them from scratches during tile work.

TROWELS

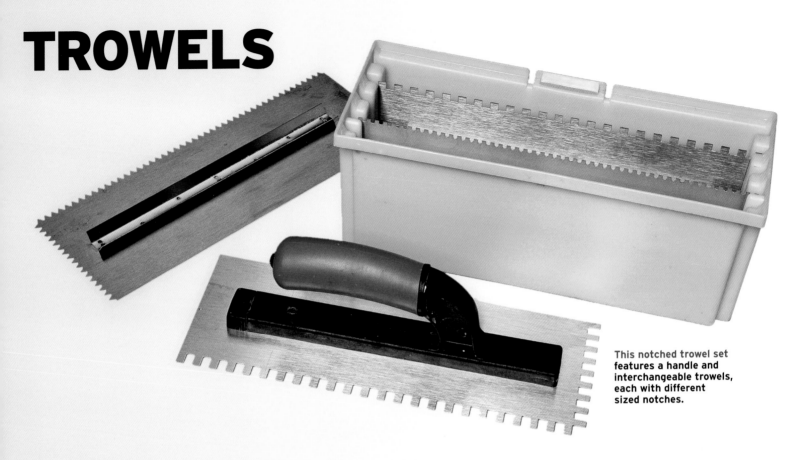

This notched trowel set features a handle and interchangeable trowels, each with different sized notches.

Trowels are used to spread thinset, mastic, and grout. Picking the right trowel for the job is essential to getting good results.

Margin trowel

Margin trowels are the preferred tool for back-buttering tiles, stirring small quantities of thinset and grout, lifting tiles from thinset, and even removing tiles during demolition. Margin trowels come in many sizes for masonry work, but one with a 2-in. by 6-in or 8-in. blade is just the right size for mixing and scooping thinset and grout for tile work.

Notched trowel

Notched trowels are the main tools used to apply thinset during the preparation process, and again when tiling. When applying thinset, hold the trowel at a 45° angle with the teeth in contact with the substrate. This keeps the thinset bed even in pattern and thickness.

➤ See "Spreading Thinset," pp. 82–83.

The trowel's long unnotched side is used for spreading the thinset on the substrate. The two notched sides, a long and a short one, are used for combing the thinset, to leave just the right amount of material for a good bond with the tile.

Notched trowels are available with notches of different sizes and shapes, such as $1/16$-in. vees and $1/2$-in. half-moons. The bigger the notch, the more thinset you apply.

A margin tool is handy for mixing small batches of materials, as well as for applying them.

While we give you advice throughout this book on which size notch to choose for a particular job, the best choice for any installation is dictated by the size of the tile and its underside pattern. Smaller, flat-bottomed tiles require less thinset and hence a smaller notch size.

Nonflat tiles, such as terra-cotta pavers and tiles with raised buttons or waffle patterns require more thinset to fill the hollow spaces under them, so you need a larger notch size. Using a trowel with notches that are too small may not leave enough thinset, which

>> >> >>

TROWELS (CONTINUED)

The smaller the notch size, the less thinset is deposited on the substrate after combing.

Applying thinset with too large a notch pattern results in excess squeeze out and messy cleanup.

The raised nubs on button-back tiles can prevent them from bonding properly with the thinset.

The full coating on the back of this tile shows that it's fully embedded in the thinset.

could lead to tile breakage. On the other hand, a trowel with too large a notch pattern leaves excess thinset that squeezes out between the tiles—a nightmare when you have to remove the excess from between each tile to leave room for grout (especially difficult with small mosaic tiles).

To set tiles with raised patterns on the back, use a large-notched trowel, such as 1/2-in. by 1/2-in. or half-moon notch. To ensure that the tiles are bonding correctly, lift an occasional tile with your margin trowel. The back should be thoroughly covered with thinset. If it isn't, switch to a trowel with larger notches, if available, or back-butter individual tiles with additional thinset.

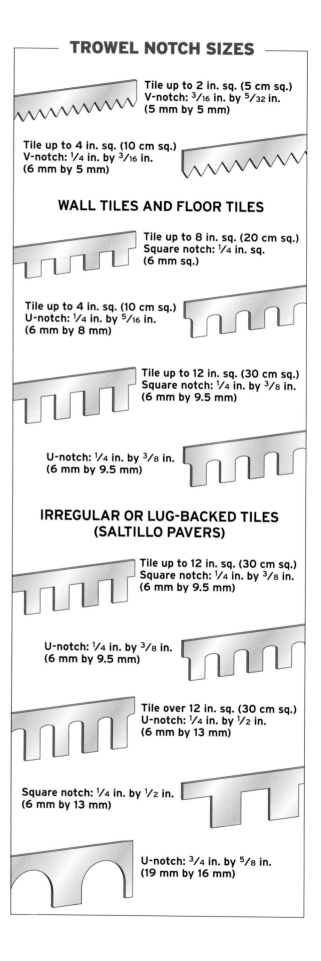

TROWEL NOTCH SIZES

Tile up to 2 in. sq. (5 cm sq.)
V-notch: 3/16 in. by 5/32 in.
(5 mm by 5 mm)

Tile up to 4 in. sq. (10 cm sq.)
V-notch: 1/4 in. by 3/16 in.
(6 mm by 5 mm)

WALL TILES AND FLOOR TILES

Tile up to 8 in. sq. (20 cm sq.)
Square notch: 1/4 in. sq.
(6 mm sq.)

Tile up to 4 in. sq. (10 cm sq.)
U-notch: 1/4 in. by 5/16 in.
(6 mm by 8 mm)

Tile up to 12 in. sq. (30 cm sq.)
Square notch: 1/4 in. by 3/8 in.
(6 mm by 9.5 mm)

U-notch: 1/4 in. by 3/8 in.
(6 mm by 9.5 mm)

IRREGULAR OR LUG-BACKED TILES (SALTILLO PAVERS)

Tile up to 12 in. sq. (30 cm sq.)
Square notch: 1/4 in. by 3/8 in.
(6 mm by 9.5 mm)

U-notch: 1/4 in. by 3/8 in.
(6 mm by 9.5 mm)

Tile over 12 in. sq. (30 cm sq.)
U-notch: 1/4 in. by 1/2 in.
(6 mm by 13 mm)

Square notch: 1/4 in. by 1/2 in.
(6 mm by 13 mm)

U-notch: 3/4 in. by 5/8 in.
(19 mm by 16 mm)

GROUTING AND CAULKING TOOLS

Grout floats are available with different compositions of rubber bottoms from hard (at left) to soft.

Like a heavy-duty pastry bag, a grout bag lets you pipe grout directly into joints.

For a consistent bead, use a caulking gun.

The tools introduced here are used to complete your tile installation. In addition to the tools described, you'll need a margin trowel, needle-nose pliers (to pull out tile spacers and wedges), buckets, scrubbers and sponges, cheesecloth (to buff off grout haze), and a sealer applicator.

➡ See "Grouting, Caulking & Sealing," pp. 212-241.

Grout float

Grout floats are for spreading and packing grout. Such floats have a rubber surface that ranges from soft to hard. For nonsanded grout, a soft rubber float spreads and sweeps off excess grout with little effort. When working with sanded grout, a hard rubber float allows you to force the heavy mixture into the joints and remove the excess.

Grout bag

Basically a large, heavy-duty pastry bag, a grout bag is used to squeeze out a large quantity of grout to fill deep joints typically used for terra-cotta floors.

Caulking gun

A caulking gun applies a steady bead of caulk, creating a flexible joint where tile meets walls, floors, and other surfaces. The thumb-operated plunger release on the gun lets you relieve pressure to the caulk cartridge to stop the flow of material when you're finished.

ANTIFRACTURE MEMBRANES

Also known as a crack-isolation membrane, antifracture membranes are liquid, paste, or sheet coverings that are applied on top of a substrate (such as drywall or concrete) before the tile is set. A membrane's main function is to prevent cracks in the substrate from radiating into the tile and causing broken and/or loose tiles. Membranes also allow for expansion and contraction in the substrate and sometimes in the tile itself. Membranes also provide a waterproof layer between the backerboard and the surface it's attached to. This helps prevent moisture from damaging, say, wood cabinets around a sink or walls around a wet area.

Always use an antifracture membrane on concrete slab floors, regardless of the type of tile to be installed. Because of earth movement under your home and the thermal expansion and contraction of the concrete, every slab floor has the potential to develop cracks over time. Floor slabs in newer homes are especially prone to developing hairline cracks due to the small gravel size (necessary for pumping concrete) and fast-drying concrete mixes used to save time during construction.

Glass tile expands and contracts at a much higher rate than does ceramic tile and stone, and its transparent nature reveals any cracks in the substrate. When glass tiles first became popular, the use of an antifracture membrane was only *suggested* by manufacturers. Now we wouldn't think of setting glass tile without a membrane underneath it.

WHAT CAN GO WRONG

Duct tape, kraft or building paper, and roofing felt of any type cannot be used as antifracture membranes. We have seen several failures of floors where someone tried to save money by gluing these materials to the floor.

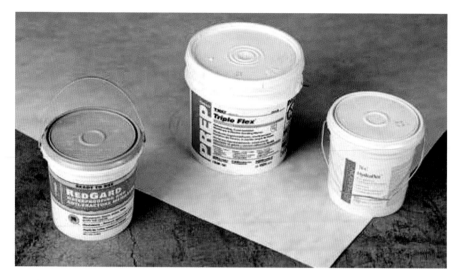

Antifracture and waterproofing membranes are available in paste and sheet types. They add to the cost of your installation but pay off in the long run by protecting the tiled surface.

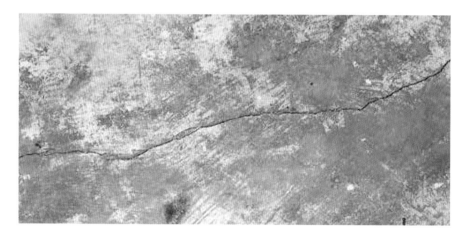

Concrete slabs are susceptible to cracking over time.

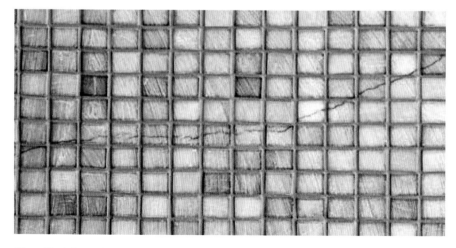

Glass tile telegraphs cracks in the substrate.

Liquid and paste membranes

Liquid- and paste-type antifracture membranes are simple to use and provide an easy way to add waterproofing to substrates being prepared for tile installation. These products are an especially good choice if you've never used a membrane product before. Some waterproofing membranes come as one-part liquids that are to ready use out of the container, whereas others are two-part pastes that require mixing before application.

One-part membranes are thick liquids that are very easy and quick to apply. RedGard®, by Custom Building Products®, has the least odor of all the liquid membrane products we've tried (however, you should still ventilate the area in which you're working). One-part membranes can be applied to counters, walls, or floors with a standard paint roller.

➡ **See "Countertop Repair and Prep," p. 119.**

Just be sure to wear gloves and work clothes when working with liquid membrane, and keep it off your skin and clothes as it clings tenaciously to any surface it touches unless you wash it off immediately.

Paste-type waterproofing membranes, such as TEC™ Triple Flex™ are two-part systems. The two components, which come in separate containers, are mixed together and then applied with a trowel. The mortar-like paste creates a very tough membrane, which works especially well to protect tile. On the downside, paste-type membranes have an extremely strong chemical odor and should be used only in properly ventilated areas. They also can take hours to dry.

>> >> >>

Mortar-type pastes create a strong membrane. Be sure to wear safety protection and use in a well-ventilated area.

One-part membranes allow you to waterproof around sinks.

TRADE SECRET

For best results, always buy tile products (thinset, grout, and so on) that bear the insignia of a national tile association, such as the Tile Council of North America® (TCNA) or the Ceramic Tile Institute of America (CTIOA). Beware of bargain, off-brand materials that lack recognized approval.

ANTIFRACTURE MEMBRANES (CONTINUED)

Sheet membranes

Resembling thin rubber, pliable sheet-type membranes are sold in rolls, like fabric yardage. Marketed under several names, including CompoSeal, sheet membranes are widely available at tile and home improvement stores. These products are rolled out, adhered to the substrate with thinset, and then flattened with a linoleum roller. A sheet membrane is a good choice if you wish to apply an antifracture membrane but want to avoid the chemical odors produced by liquid and paste membranes. Just make sure that the particular material you buy is approved for use with ceramic tile.

Another type of sheet membrane is Schluter-DITRA uncoupling membrane. Like other membranes, it allows for normal horizontal movement of the substrate on a floor, which helps prevent cracks in the tile and grout. In the case of Schluter-DITRA, the "uncoupling" is a descriptive word for the way the membrane or cells on their orange waffle mat achieve the necessary separation between tile and substrate. However, Schluter-DITRA has the advantage that it is polyethylene, rather than a latex product, which makes it an important option for those with chemical sensitivities. The membrane is also installed with nonlatex modified thinset and may also be used for waterproofing.

A sheet membrane **is adhered to the substrate with thinset.**

An uncoupling membrane is another type of antifracture and waterproofing membrane. You'll need a utility knife to cut the membrane and a notched trowel and wood float, followed by a weighted roller, to thinset the membrane in place.

BACKERBOARD AND OTHER SUBSTRATES

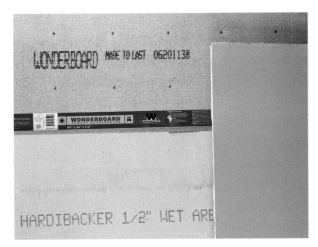

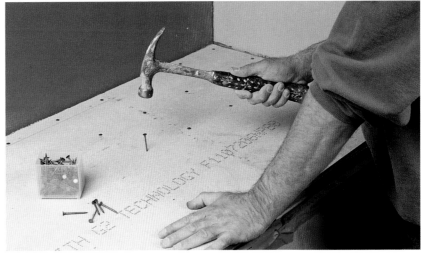

Backerboard is the substrate **of choice for many durable installations: (clockwise from top) WonderBoard®, DensShield®, and Hardiboard®.**

Backerboard can be nailed **or screwed into plywood or studs.**

Backerboard is cement-based board that can be fastened with nails or screws. It provides a substrate stable enough to support a long-lasting tile job. Applied over wood cabinets, drywall, or plywood floors, it provides a terrific alternative to installing tile over a traditional mud bed, a job that requires considerable skill and is too involved for all but the most diehard DIYers.

Sold under several brand names, backerboards come in ¼-in. and ½-in. thicknesses. Choosing the right thickness allows you to install a substrate that matches the height of surrounding surfaces—for example, aligning a tiled floor with an existing hardwood or carpeted floor or a tiled counter with an adjacent wooden bar counter.

For a durable installation, all types of backerboard must be set in thinset, fastened in place with nails or screws, and taped to reinforce the gaps between sheets.

> → See "Installing Backerboard on Floors," p. 123.

Backerboard can't be used to level or flatten a bumpy floor or counter. And, with the exception of DensShield, backerboards are not fully waterproof, only water resistant.

WonderBoard

WonderBoard is composed of cement aggregate sandwiched between two layers of fiberglass mesh. It was the first backerboard on the market and is still around today, which is a sure sign of a reliable product. It is sold in 3-ft. by 5-ft. sheets. WonderBoard is a bit harder to cut and is heavier than other backerboards, making it a bit more cumbersome to work with.

Hardiboard

Also available in 3-ft. by 5-ft. sheets, Hardiboard brand backerboard is made of cement and ground sand. Although it looks more like layered cardboard, Hardiboard is a very strong material that's approved by all tile certification agencies. It is lightweight and easy to cut with a saw or by scoring and snapping. It's such a trouble-free product, that we recommend it for DIYers who are installing backerboard for the first time.

DensShield

DensShield is a board composed of gypsum and fiberglass mat with an acrylic coating. This is one of the only backerboards that is truly waterproof, which makes it ideal for wet locations like tub and shower enclosures. Available only in ½-in.-thick sheets, DensShield is more expensive than other backerboards. But if you are concerned about waterproofing, this is the right choice. There are specific requirements for using this product in a watertight installation. (Check the manufacturer's literature.) Be aware that you can't use DensShield on a floor with tiles smaller than 2 in. sq.   >> >> >>

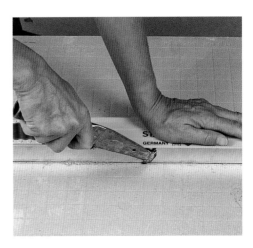

To cut backerboard, **score it, then snap along the score line.**

BACKERBOARD AND OTHER SUBSTRATES (CONTINUED)

As tile technology continues to adapt and evolve, new materials are developed that make DIY projects easier. Backerboard is not the only substitute for a traditional mud substrate. Some of the alternatives are also great at solving particular problems.

Wedi® board

Wedi board is one of the only waterproof backerboards on the market. When installed with Wedi's sealant adhesive, your floor or wall will be completely sealed from water. It is so lightweight and easy to cut that it makes an ideal substrate for mosaics or other craft tile projects.

Self-leveling compounds

Self-leveling compounds are used to flatten out floors that are uneven or out of level to prepare them for tile installation. In addition to being unpleasant to walk on, lumpy floors make doing a good tile-setting job difficult. Tiles end up looking uneven when laid on top of a wavy surface and may not get bonded properly.

You mix the powdered self-leveling compound with water, then pour it over a wood or concrete floor. The compound, which can be poured up to 2 in. thick, seeks its own level and dries flat and true. Self-leveling compounds have a relatively short working time before they go off (begin to harden), so it's best to partition your uneven floor into small areas and pour each section separately. About 4 hours later, you'll have a floor that is rock hard, flat, and level.

➡ See "Applying Self-Leveling Compound," p. 110.

Wedi building panels are 100% waterproof, light, and robust and can be applied to practically any substrate, making them an ideal base for tile.

Self-leveling compound is mixed with water.

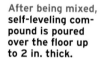

After being mixed, self-leveling compound is poured over the floor up to 2 in. thick.

CHOOSING AN ADHESIVE

There are many ways to adhere tile permanently to backerboard and other substrates. While mastics and epoxies have their place in some applications, thinset mortars are by far the most popular products for DIY tile installations.

Thinset is a powdered cement and sand mixture that, when combined with water or fortifying additives, creates a strong mortar adhesive that's terrific for bonding tile. When used correctly, thinset creates an inseparable bond between tiles and substrates.

Thinsets are typically sold in 25-lb. or 50-lb. bags. The amount of thinset you'll need depends on the size of the tile you're installing and the notch size of the trowel you use to spread the thinset. See "Thinset Coverage" on p. 80 to help you estimate the amount you'll need.

There are a wide array of thinset products, including standard, medium-bed, fast-setting, and flexible varieties. (There's even a special thinset just for setting black and green marble!) Each of these products is described in the following sections, to help you choose the right one for your particular installation. »» »» »»

TRADE SECRET

Acrylic in liquid form is often called latex. When it is included in a manufactured product as a dry material, it is called polymer modified. Both have the same properties; they're just different compositions.

Thinset mortars **are the main adhesive for tile installations.**

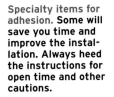

Always use white thinset **for glass tile so the color of the tile isn't changed by the adhesive beneath.**

Specialty items for adhesion. **Some will save you time and improve the installation. Always heed the instructions for open time and other cautions.**

For repairs or small projects, premixed mortars and grouts are available. Although they cost a bit more per square foot, there is less mess and no mixing involved.

CHOOSING AN ADHESIVE (CONTINUED)

Some thinsets require **an acrylic additive, giving superior bonding strength.**

Large floor tiles require large-format thinset to support the weight and aid in leveling the tile.

Standard thinset

Standard thinset is basic adhesive mortar that can be used to set all standard white-bodied or porous tiles. Adding acrylic admix to this thinset, instead of water, gives the mortar much greater strength and makes a mixture that's right for setting any kind of tile, including porcelain and glass.

Thinset comes in either white or gray, depending on the cement color used in the manufacturing process. Your choice of thinset color should be based on the color of your grout: Use white thinset with lighter-colored grouts and gray thinset with darker-colored grouts. When installing translucent or transparent tiles, such as white marble and glass, always use white thinset so that the tiles will maintain their true color.

Fortified thinset and acrylic additives

A fortified (or modified) thinset is just like standard thinset, except that it contains an acrylic additive to increase its strength. You can also make your own fortified thinset

mortar, if you wish, by mixing standard thinset powder with an acrylic additive, such as Acrylbond®, instead of water.

Fortified mortars are good for any tile installation in which extra bonding strength is required, say when setting tiles that absorb moisture slowly (and hence, slow the drying and curing process), including glass, porcelain, and vitrified tiles as well as natural stone tiles.

Large-format thinset

Large-format thinset has properties that make it great for setting big floor tiles. It is mixed with a larger-grain-size sand, so it does not compress like standard thinset. When you set large, heavy tiles into this robust thinset (20-in.-sq. paver tiles can weigh over 10 lb. each), it will not sag or allow tiles to droop. This is crucial when leveling tiles one to the other, a necessary step to achieve a flat floor. Another big advantage with this thinset is that it prevents larger tiles from sagging on a wall.

⚠ **WARNING**

Acrylic-fortified thinsets bond strongly not only to tile but also to everything they come in contact with. Keep your work area scrupulously clean and have a water bucket and sponge handy to wipe thinset off the edges and faces of the tiles right after setting them. Keep your hands clean or expect to find thinset bonded to your fingernails. (If you end up with dried thinset on your tile, use an acrylic grout haze cleaner to remove it.)

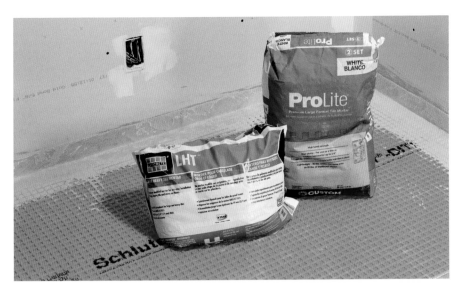

With the popularity of large-format tiles, manufacturers have formulated thinsets with larger-grain-size sand to minimize sagging and slumping. These large-format thinsets help to keep wall tiles from sliding while setting and keep floor tiles smooth and flat.

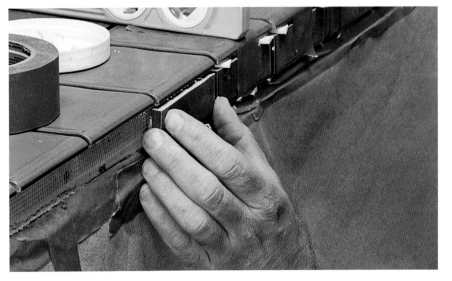

Quick-setting adhesives **work well for tiling vertical surfaces.**

Fast-setting thinset

Fast-setting fortified thinsets such as Speed-Set™ allow you to install tile and grout on the same day. These products are convenient for commercial projects and high-traffic areas because they offer minimal downtime from productivity. They are also a great choice when setting tile on the edges of countertops and other vertical surfaces. If adhered with standard slow-drying thinset, vertical tiles could slip out of place, especially if jarred.

Fast-setting thinset has a short open time (20 minutes to 30 minutes), so it's best to mix and apply in small batches. It sets firm enough to allow grouting in about 4 hours (though grout still needs between 12 hours and 3 days to cure, depending on the type of grout you choose). Fast-setting thinset also provides great convenience when setting tiles in a household entry or other doorway, as it allows you to walk on those tiles only a few hours after they're set.

Flexible thinset

As unlikely as it sounds, there's actually a flexible thinset that, despite being a concrete product, remains flexible after it has cured.

This makes it a good choice for bonding tile over areas of substrate prone to cracking (say, a concrete floor) in place of an antifracture membrane. Flexible mortar is also good for setting small areas of glass tile. This saves time and trouble by allowing you to set a few glass liners or accent tiles surrounded by ceramic tiles, without having to apply an antifracture membrane to just those small areas.

Green and black marble thinset

Unlike other types of marble tile, green and black marble are moisture sensitive. If you

>> >> >>

CAULK

Caulk is a flexible acrylic latex or silicone material that's used to seal the seams between tiled surfaces (shower walls, corners of backsplashes) between tile and fixtures (faucets, kitchen sinks), and wherever tile meets other materials—butcherblock, paneled walls, and so on. Caulk is used in place of grout in these areas because its flexibility allows the different surfaces or materials to move independently. Such natural expansion and contraction causes inflexible grout to crack.

Types of caulk

Between the two major types of caulk, silicone is the better choice in wet areas and for outdoor projects. However, it is much more difficult to apply than latex caulk, and residue must be cleaned up with a solvent. Latex caulk cleans up with soap and water. There are some latex-silicone caulk blends that combine the benefits of both products. Most caulks are available to match grout colors, both in sanded and nonsanded textures that blend easily with the look of the grout.

➡ See "Applying Caulk," p. 236.

Expansion joint foam

If your floor tile is very thick, you will create deep expansion joints (over $3/8$ in. deep) around the perimeter of a room. These joints will need backing before you can caulk them. Expansion joint foam comes in both rolls and rods and is a good backing material for partially filling a grout joint ahead of topping it off with caulk.

➡ See "Expansion Joints in Tile Floors," p. 238.

Apply caulk in a continuous smooth bead.

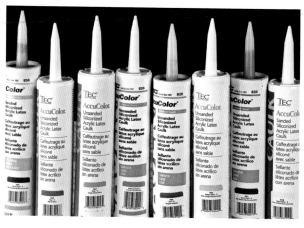

Caulk is the flexible solution for areas of movement in your tile job. Caulk colors are available to match your grout.

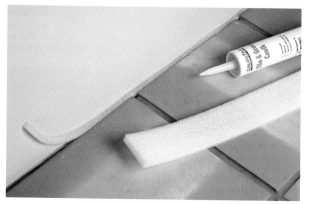

Expansion foam comes in rolls and can be easily cut to any width to fit the depth of the grout joints before adding caulk.

Caulk is used to fill expansion joints around a room.

HARDWARE AND TAPE

A Fiberglass tape with adhesive helps bridge gaps, for a long lasting backerboard installation.

B Screws for attaching backerboard are alkali resistant and have ridges to recess the head.

C Use special nails to secure backerboard.

D Apply tape smoothly without bumps or ridges.

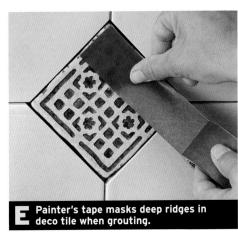

E Painter's tape masks deep ridges in deco tile when grouting.

U p until now, this chapter has outlined the most important materials you'll need for a typical tile installation, such as backerboard, thinset, grout, caulk, and sealer. However, there are other hardware items that you'll likely need for a tile job: joint tape, nails and screws, and wedges and spacers **A**. You may also need edge trim designed to work specifically with tile. These transition materials will put the finishing touches on your installation.

Unlike regular screws and nails, the fasteners designed for attaching backerboard to walls and counters are strong and alkali resistant. In contrast, standard drywall screws tend to break, and vinyl-coated construction nails can rust. Backerboard screws have a bugle head with ridges that cut into

the board to recess the head **B**. You can also use nails to attach backerboard **C**, but screws are more secure, and there is less likelihood of cracking the board with a misplaced blow.

Joint tape

Made of a fiberglass mesh, joint tape is applied over joints between sheets of backerboard to bridge the gaps. It helps consolidate different pieces of the substrate into a single structure that will not crack or move. There are two choices in joint tape. One is sold specifically for use with backerboard but has no adhesive. Instead, we prefer to use the self-adhesive yellow tape that's a favorite of drywall installers. It doesn't always stick firmly by itself (especially when you try to

wrap it around counter edges). But once it's set in place with thinset **D** we find that it's easier to use than the nonadhesive tape.

Painter's tape

Although not specifically a tiling material, painter's tape has a wide variety of uses in a tile installation. Use it to mask areas you don't want covered with caulk or grout **E**, secure rosin paper or plastic tarps, or prevent splitting or damage around the cut surfaces of backerboard. Use blue tape specifically meant for painting rather than regular masking tape. Painter's tape is more resistant to moisture and pulls away without damaging surfaces.

TILE SPACERS AND WEDGES

Available from tile supply stores and home centers, tile spacers provide a handy means of spacing and adjusting tiles during installation. Made of flexible plastic, spacers set between tiles help keep them evenly spaced, producing grout joints of even width Ⓐ.

Tile spacers are sized by the grout joint they'll create—from 1/16 in. all the way up to 1/2 in. They come in two styles: X-shaped spacers are used in the junction between four tiles; T-shaped spacers are used where three tiles meet, as between field tile and trim or tiles laid in a brick or other alternating pattern.

Another kind of spacer, U-shaped spacers Ⓑ, are made of hard plastic and are very useful for leveling a plywood rough top on countertops before installing backerboard. We consider them to be far superior to wood wedges as they are flat and come in three thicknesses: 1/16 in., 1/8 in., 1/4 in. These sizes allow for almost any counter leveling job. You can usually find U-shaped spacers at marble or granite supply warehouses.

Special tile-setting wedges Ⓒ made of flexible, soft plastic are very handy for fine-tuning the position and alignment of tiles applied to vertical surfaces. You can use them either as adjusters to lift tiles as necessary or as spacers between tiles. For handmade, uneven tiles, you may even use two wedges stacked together for spacing purposes.

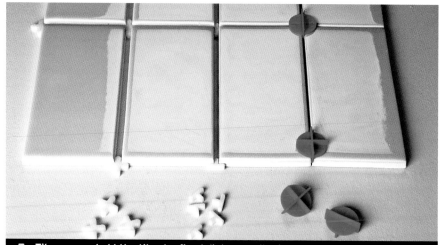

A Tile spacers hold the tile at a fixed distance, allowing you to create regular even grout lines.

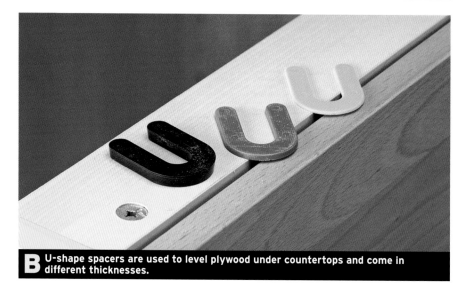

B U-shape spacers are used to level plywood under countertops and come in different thicknesses.

Use small flexible wedges to adjust the alignment of tiles on a vertical surface.

ATHENA TILE & IMPORTS
450 WEDGES
18271 Parthenia St. • Northridge, CA 91325
Phone: (818) 993-5807 • Fax (818) 993-3431

C Use small flexible wedges to adjust the alignment of tiles on a vertical surface.

Leveling clips

Leveling clips or spacers are another type of grout joint spacer, usually part of a "system" that enables you to lift large-format tiles in relation to one another, basically to level adjacent tiles. You cannot prevent lippage caused by warped tiles, but leveling clips will "level the playing field," so to speak, by giving you the flattest floors and walls possible. Leveling clips are valuable and necessary time savers if you plan to work with large-format tiles.

There are a multitude of manufacturers for varied types of leveling systems, and all of them do the job. Some clips require a specialized gun type of tool to tighten them, some twist into place, and some are locked in with a wedge. All perform the same task of leveling adjacent tiles to one another. Also, some systems have clips or spacers of varying widths to provide the grout joint size you desire. If you have a one-size clip leveling system and you want to install with a bigger grout joint, you can use traditional spacers (T- or X-shape) in the appropriate size.

Leveling clip systems are important **for installation of large-format tiles, and there are many varieties, both in size and type of system. Shown here, from left to right: gun and cap, wedge with one-size leveler, screw-type with various-size levelers, and wedge with various-size levelers.**

If the system you choose offers only one grout joint size, you can make a larger joint by inserting a traditional spacer at the intersections.

HOW LEVELING CLIPS WORK

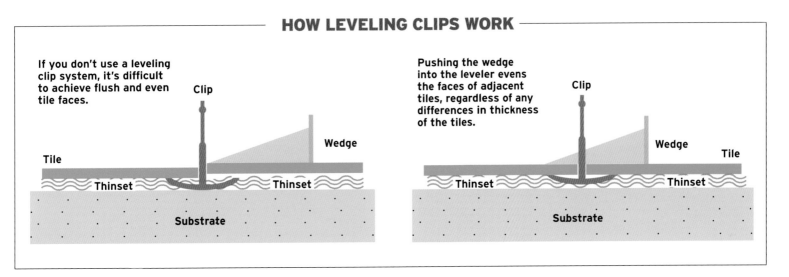

If you don't use a leveling clip system, it's difficult to achieve flush and even tile faces.

Clip

Wedge

Tile

Thinset   Thinset

Substrate

Pushing the wedge into the leveler evens the faces of adjacent tiles, regardless of any differences in thickness of the tiles.

Clip

Wedge

Tile

Thinset   Thinset

Substrate

TRANSITION AND EDGE TRIM

A hallmark of a professional floor tile installation is the way the tile meets other surfaces. The transition between tile and a wood, linoleum, or carpeted floor should be clean and seamless. Fortunately, there are metal trim strips specifically designed to create such a smooth transition **A**. Available at most tile supply stores, trim strips come in copper, stainless steel, gold, and other finishes. The trim (the Schluter system is shown here) comes in several types, each designed to work for a particular application—for example, where tile meets carpeting **B**, wood or linoleum at the same height **C**, and flooring at a different height **D**.

Threshold

Threshold strips are used to create a transition between tile and other kinds of flooring in entries and doorways **E**.

Available in wood or metal and in a wide variety of shapes and sizes, threshold is easy to screw down into the wood subflooring. It not only covers the unsightly seam between, say, a tile and wood floor, but can also make up for any height difference between different kinds of flooring. You'll find the best selection of wood threshold pieces at a hardwood flooring store.

A Schluter edges can bridge the area between your new tile and any other floor surface or can be used as an edge detail.

B Trim was used here to transition between tile and carpeting.

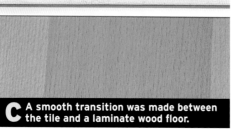

C A smooth transition was made between the tile and a laminate wood floor.

D This trim makes the transition when two floor surfaces are at different heights.

E Threshold strips are used in doorways and passages.

Edge trims used to come only in basic metal finish colors, but now they are available in an array of nonmetallic colors as well.

Metal edging can frame **and delineate a shower niche for a modern look.**

Edge trim

More and more tiles, especially large-format tiles, do not have an accompanying bullnose or other trim piece. Or if they do have trim, it might not be a good match. A growing trend in recent years is an alternative choice of slim edge trims (plastic and metal), which are available in many different colors, profiles, and sizes. Some trim pieces may match the fixtures in a room, adding an elegant or a modern streamlined feature. You can use these trims for outside corners (where two tiles meet) to frame a niche as tile base for a floor, or as a transition from tile to another material.

You can frame or finish **any opening with metal edging.**

PROTECTING THE WORK AREA

Preparing an area for tile work always generates lots of dust and debris, especially if you must remove an old counter, floor, or backsplash. Protecting the area around your project will save the rest of your home from accidental damage and will make cleanup much faster, too. Rolls of plastic and plastic tarps come in different thicknesses and are great for keeping dust off appliances and furniture. Plastic also works well to seal doorways to keep dust out of rooms and areas adjacent to your work space. Just measure the plastic to fit the doorway and tape it down to the floor ❶.

Then add a towel at the floor for added protection ❷. The towel will add additional weight to hold the plastic in place in case air drafts cause the plastic to billow in and out.

When taping down plastic tarps or protective paper, use blue painter's tape ❸, which is easier to remove than regular masking tape and usually doesn't damage the underlying surface. However, we have seen blue tape damage wallpaper, paint, and even tile sealer, so to be safe, test tape surfaces before application. Duct tape is the right tape to use in areas that may get wet or that require heavy-duty protection, as in high-traffic areas. Duct tape can leave a residue over time so don't leave it (or any other tape) in place for a prolonged period.

1 Taping plastic sheeting over a doorway keeps out dust.

2 A towel at the doorway will secure the plastic sheeting.

3 Tape plastic sheeting to the door frame using blue painter's tape.

TRADE SECRET

It's a good idea to remove any paintings, china plates, and other objects that are hanging in the demo area, or leaning against the other side of the wall. When in doubt, move it out.

SETTING UP A WORK SPACE

A garage can be an ideal place to set up a work space and staging area. It gives you a spot to safely store tile, tools, and materials, with easy access to both the outdoors (for mixing and cleanup) and the job area inside your home.

Just remember that many tile materials (grout, caulk) must be kept at moderate temperatures. Move them inside if garage temperatures get too hot or too cold. Use large plastic tarps to protect the walls and floors from spills and water spray (if you set up a water saw).

Although better done outside, you can mix powdered materials, such as thinset and grout, inside your garage as long as you wear a dust mask and leave the garage door open. Just keep in mind that mixing and cutting will layer the area with fine dust.

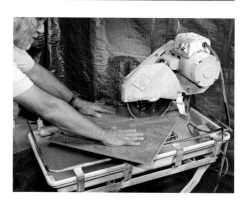

A large plastic tarp helps protect your garage work space from wet-saw spray, thinset splatters, and other messes.

PROTECTING FLOORS

It's surprising how easy it is to track even the smallest amount of dust or dirt around on the bottoms of your shoes. Cloth tarps are a great invention to keep you from trailing things in and out of your work area, especially over carpeted areas. We like the tarps that painters use, which come in long strips 4 ft. wide. They work well down hallways and are wide enough to provide protection for walkways leading to your job area **Ⓐ**. To protect finished floors, put down rosin paper (a heavy-duty rose-colored paper that comes in rolls), then cover it with sheets of Masonite®, thin plywood, or other paneling **Ⓑ**. The Masonite also provides good protection if you need to roll out heavy appliances, such as refrigerators and dishwashers. The rosin paper helps protect the underlying floor from debris that gets trapped underneath the Masonite.

To prepare for a kitchen floor demo, first unplug all appliances and disconnect stoves and ranges from gas lines. Before moving a refrigerator, disconnect the water line for the refrigerator's icemaker. When moving appliances out of the room, use a sturdy dolly or hand truck covered with a blanket (to prevent scratches) **Ⓒ**. Set the appliances atop plywood to prevent damage to the storage area's floor. Always tape down a tarp or towel at the doorway of the room you're working in to protect the flooring, catch debris, and give you a place to wipe your feet as you leave the area **Ⓓ**.

⚠ WARNING
Make sure to cover smoke alarms within range of your demolition area with a plastic bag or plastic sheeting wrapped with blue tape. The dust raised can trigger false alarms.

Ⓐ **Cloth tarps** can provide invaluable protection for finished floors when walking back and forth to the job area.

Ⓑ **Rosin paper** covered by Masonite provides thorough protection for any finished floor.

Ⓒ Hand trucks make it easy to lift heavy, awkward objects.

Ⓓ Tape a towel or tarp to the carpeting to prevent soiling it.

REMOVING TILE FROM A BACKSPLASH

1 Carefully use a hammer and chisel to remove edge tiles.

2 A margin trowel may also be used to lift or pull tiles away from the wall.

3 Carefully remove backsplash tiles, to prevent excessive damage to the drywall.

If you need to remove old tile from the backsplash, start by prying up any edge trim or edge tiles **1**. Place your chisel between the grouted edge and the wall. If the tile is set directly to the wall, the tiles should come off easily when pried with a margin trowel **2**. If the tile is over a mud bed, it'll take more effort to remove the old backsplash. You can try using a prybar or hammer claw to get under the tiles and pry them off **3**. To avoid punching holes in the wall surface, try to restrict heavy prying to areas where the wallboard is attached to studs.

PREPPING CONCRETE FLOORS

1 Tile installed on a concrete floor with old mastic left on it won't bond properly and, eventually, will come loose.

2 Chemical floor strippers make short work of removing glue and other debris from your floor to prepare for a new tile installation.

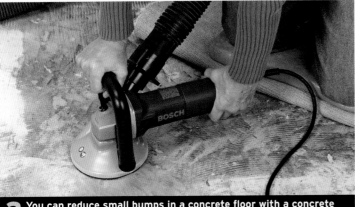

3 You can reduce small bumps in a concrete floor with a concrete grinder, connected to a shop vacuum to reduce dust output.

4 Use your level to check the concrete slab for hills or valleys before you start any tile work.

Once a floor has been taken down to bare concrete, it's essential to remove all paint, glue, and other residue from the slab before installing tile. If the surface isn't clean, you may end up with loose tiles that require removal and replacement **1**. Scrape off old paint with a scraper fitted with a sharp blade. If you have trouble removing glue residue, try using a chemical stripper (preferably one of the newer, less-toxic types with a citric-acid base) **2**. After stripping, rinse the floor to eliminate any remaining residue that may interfere with the tile adhesive bonding. Another way to remove old glue, vinyl backing, or other sticky stuff is by grinding it away with a portable angle grinder fitted with a 4-in. carbide/diamond grinder cup wheel. If the machine has a dust port, connect it to a portable shop vacuum to reduce the dust **3**. If you'd rather leave this dirty job to someone else, there are professional companies that will clean the surface for you (search online for "Concrete Restoration or Repairs").

Checking concrete for flatness

For a good installation, the concrete floor under the tile must be flat. Tiles don't bend, and big tiles (16 in. sq. and larger) are very difficult to install properly on uneven concrete. Flatness is even more important when setting mosaic tiles and close-fitting large tiles. Small mosaic tiles follow every hill and dale of an uneven floor, creating a sand dune appearance. Large tiles set with narrow grout joints on an uneven floor will create lippage, meaning the tile edges aren't flush with one another. Lippage not only looks bad, but it also can pose a significant tripping hazard.

To check the floor for flatness, lay a long level or straightedge across different areas of the floor and mark any humps or valleys **4**. Don't worry if the level's bubble shows that the floor isn't perfectly level—flatness is more important. The easiest way to smooth an undulating floor is with a self-leveling compound.

➔ See "Applying Self-Leveling Compound," p. 110.

You can reduce small bumps and larger high spots with an angle grinder fitted with a masonry cup wheel or with a chipping hammer fitted with a flat-tipped chisel **5** (on p. 110). Fill low spots with regular thinset, spreading and then feathering the material to create a smooth, even surface **6** (on p. 110).

>> >> >>

PREPPING CONCRETE FLOORS (CONTINUED)

5 Use a chipping hammer to remove excess concrete from high spots or small hills.

6 Fill and feather low spots with thinset. Spread with a flat trowel, then smooth and check with a straightedge.

APPLYING SELF-LEVELING COMPOUND

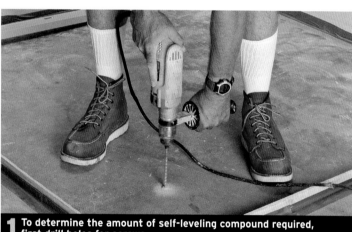

1 To determine the amount of self-leveling compound required, first drill holes for screws.

2 Tap plastic anchors into the holes.

S elf-leveling compound is a thin concrete mixture that's designed to be poured over a bumpy concrete slab (or an uneven wood subfloor) to flatten and level it in preparation for tiling. Each bag covers 50 sq. ft. up to $1/8$ in. deep.

To establish how deep you'll need to pour the compound to level your floor, drill $1/4$-in. holes into the floor, spaced a few feet apart in each direction **1**. Put a screw anchor in each hole and drive in a $1\frac{1}{2}$-in. drywall screw **2**. Use your level to find the high point on the floor and raise the highest screw until its head is about

WHAT CAN GO WRONG

Some two-story homes have lightweight concrete floors upstairs. These floors contain gypsum, which can swell and pull moisture out of tile-setting materials, causing them to set too quickly. You can't use self-leveling compounds over lightweight concrete, and setting tile directly on it can cause cracking. To tile these floors, consult a tile professional.

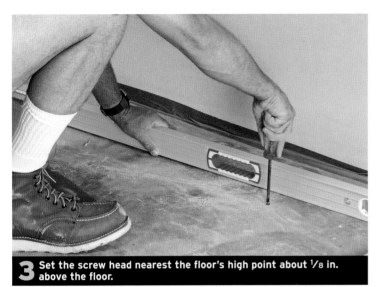

3 Set the screw head nearest the floor's high point about 1/8 in. above the floor.

4 Adjust the screws so that all the heads are level with each other across the floor.

5 Seal off the wall edges, holes, and openings with duct tape.

6 Tape wood strips together to use as dividers to separate areas.

7 Apply primer to the floor with a roller and allow it to dry.

1/8 in. above the concrete **3**. Adjust all adjacent screws until they're level with the high-point screw **4**. Work your way around the floor, adjusting each screw until they are all level with each other. You'll need to pour enough compound to just cover the heads of these screws.

To ensure a good bond between the self-leveling compound and the concrete, clean the floor thoroughly with a sponge and water. After the floor dries, use duct tape in joints between the walls and the floor **5** as well as around any toilet flanges, pipes, or other lines that pass through the concrete. Use duct tape to hold a scrap piece of wood across any doorway. The compound is very runny when it's poured, so press the tape in place firmly. We recommend that you don't pour more than 25 sq. ft. of self-leveler at a time. Larger areas are best treated in several pours. To create a form for the pour area, tape lath wood strips to the floor **6**.

Next, use a 1/4-in.-nap paint roller to apply a coat of latex concrete primer to the pour area **7** and let it dry for about an hour. Set up three 5-gal. pails and measure the required amount of water (specified on the compound's bag) into each one **8** (on p. 112). Depending on the size of the area and depth of the pour, mix two or three pails worth of material **9** (it's better to mix more than to come up short). If the pour requires more than three bags of material, mix and pour two bags, and let it firm up for about an hour. Then mix and pour the remainder. Pour any excess material into other areas

>> >> >>

APPLYING SELF-LEVELING COMPOUND (CONTINUED)

8 Use an accurate measuring container to add the proper amount of water.

9 Pour dry compound into the water-filled bucket slowly. Mix with a low-speed drill.

10 The poured compound starts to spread and seek its own level.

11 Use a long-handled hoe to help spread compound into the corners.

12 Shake out a small amount of sand to stop any leaks from the self-leveler.

13 After the floor has dried, lift the wood strips with the claw end of a hammer.

you need to level (if any), to get a head start on your next pour.

Mix the compound outdoors because of the dust, and wear a dust mask. Stir the compound for two minutes with an electric drill fitted with a mixer, and pour it into your form until the liquid is even with the screw heads **10**. Use a gardener's hoe to help spread the liquid **11**, but don't work it too much once it has found its level. If the mix seeps through the taped areas, pour some sand on the leak to stop it. Sweep up

the excess after the compound has dried **12**. Allow the leveler to dry for a half hour, then pull the lath strips **13** and start a new area, as needed. Level each newly poured area to the previous hardened area, so your whole floor will be the same height. Once all areas are poured, you're ready to tile on a perfectly flat and level surface.

TRADE SECRET
Pouring self-leveling compound is easier when two people do it. You'll need to move quickly during the pour and clean up your tools quickly afterward.

APPLYING AN ANTIFRACTURE MEMBRANE

E ven flat, smooth, and level concrete floors can crack many years after they're poured, and those cracks can telegraph through tile.

Simple and inexpensive to apply, antifracture membranes can prevent this problem. Membranes come in three types: paste, sheet, and two-part. Each has qualities that make it better for some situations than for others.

➡ See "Choosing an Adhesive," pp. 77-80.

Paste-type membranes are very easy to apply and are a good choice for slabs that lack cracks and gaps. After cleaning the floor ❶, protect your baseboard and any cabinets or fixed furniture by taping them off with blue painter's tape ❷. Use a ³/₄-in.-nap paint roller to apply the viscous liquid to your floor, making sure to cover the area well ❸ (on p. 114). After the membrane has dried for 24 hours, remove the tape, and the surface is ready for tile.

Sheet-type membranes are good for bridging large cracks in a concrete floor. They can also be used to prevent cracking problems in areas where the concrete meets other floor materials, such as wood ❹. After cutting the membrane sheet to size, spread a layer of latex-modified thinset over the floor, using a ¼-in. by ¼-in. notched trowel ❺. Lay the sheet on top of the fresh thinset

❻ and use the flat side of the notched trowel to force it into the thinset. Then use the flat side once again to feather edge the thinset that squeezes out, making a nice transition from membrane to concrete. Finally, use some tiles to weight the sheet down until it firms up, usually about an hour ❼. This helps prevent curling of the membrane edges.

Two-part membranes are made up of two pastes mixed together before application. Good for dealing with surface cracks, these membranes have more body than paste-type membranes and apply almost as easily. But because they emit toxic fumes, you'll need to wear an approved respirator and ventilate your work area well.

➡ See "Personal Safety Gear," pp. 42-43.

Start by filling cracks ⅛ in. or wider with epoxy filler made for concrete repairs ❽. After mixing the membrane per the instructions on the packaging, use a ³/₁₆-in. by ³/₁₆-in. V-notched trowel to spread it on the concrete. As with thinset, first use the flat side of the trowel to spread it over the concrete, ensuring a tenacious bond ❾. Then use the notched side to get a consistent membrane thickness ❿. Finally, use a steel concrete finishing float to smooth down the ridges, leaving a flat, even surface that's ready for tile ⓫. >> >> >>

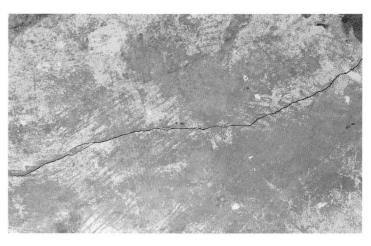

Most concrete slabs **eventually develop cracks. Antifracture membranes prevent cracks from creating problems with tile installed over concrete.**

1 Remove surface debris with a wet sponge before applying an antifracture membrane.

2 Tape off the baseboard to protect it from a paste antifracture membrane.

APPLYING AN ANTIFRACTURE MEMBRANE (CONTINUED)

3 Apply paste antifracture membrane to a floor using a long-handled roller.

4 A sheet-type antifracture membrane is applied to cover a 2x4 embedded in the concrete in a doorway area.

5 Trowel modified thinset over the entire area before applying the membrane.

6 Apply sheet membrane and use the flat trowel to embed it in the thinset.

7 Weight down the sheet membrane to prevent curling as it dries.

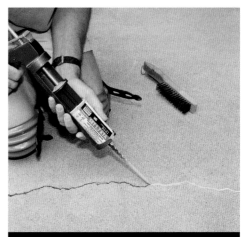

8 Use concrete epoxy to fill any crack over ⅛ in. wide before applying a two-part antifracture membrane.

9 Wear a respirator to protect yourself from two-part membranes.

10 Comb the membrane in one direction using a ³/₁₆-in. V-notched trowel.

11 Smooth the ridges of the combed surface with a flat trowel.

INSTALLING SCHLUTER-DITRA MEMBRANE

Homes today are more insulated and isolated from the outside environment than ever before. Although this saves us a lot of money on energy bills, it means that chemicals in our environment and our homes become trapped inside and people with chemical sensitivities may suffer adverse reactions. If you have environmental concerns, you may wish to use an uncoupling membrane, which allows you to install porcelain tile without the need for latex-enhanced adhesives.

The Schluter-DITRA mat allows air to circulate beneath the tile, which helps the thinset cure thoroughly yet gives you a strong bond without chemical additives. A membrane like DITRA does not outgas like solvent-based membranes do, and thus will not release chemicals into your living space.

Lay out the mat and cut it to length (mats come in 39-in. widths and varying lengths). Mark the outside edge of the mat with a pencil, which will tell you where to apply the thinset ❶. Roll the mat out of the way and then dampen and wipe clean the substrate with a sponge and clean water; this will help the thinset cure more slowly and not set up too quickly by losing moisture to a dry slab ❷,❸. Make sure there's no standing water.

Mix the nonlatex modified thinset wetter than normal but with enough body to still hold a notch. Comb the thinset in parallel lines with a ¼-in. by ¼-in. notched trowel ❹ and immediately roll the membrane back in place ❺. Force the DITRA into the mortar bed with a wood float ❻ or a weighted roller ❼ (on p. 116). Now roll the remaining mat up onto the

>> >> >>

1 After cutting the membrane to size, mark the edge as a guide for spreading thinset.

2 Wipe down the area to remove any dust and debris.

3 Dampen the entire surface right before spreading the thinset.

4 Spread nonlatex modified thinset, keeping the notches parallel to avoid air pockets.

5 Roll out the DITRA mat on the thinset, following the pencil line drawn earlier.

6 Embed the membrane into the thinset by pressing down on the wood float across the entire surface.

INSTALLING SCHLUTER-DITRA MEMBRANE (CONTINUED)

area you just completed. Dampen, clean the substrate once again, comb out more thinset **8**, roll out the mat as you go, and embed it in place. Lay each new section of DITRA side by side without overlap until the floor area is completely covered.

7 Alternatively, you might wish to use a weighted roller to embed the membrane.

8 Dampen the next section of the substrate, apply more thinset, and comb in one direction before continuing to roll out more membrane.

INSTALLING KERDI BAND

Kerdi Band is a waterproof strip that allows you to maintain waterproofing integrity so that if you had a major leak, water would not wick up the wall or in between the DITRA sheets.

Once you've finished laying the DITRA mat, snap a line 2½ in. above the mat (or use a laser level) **1**, **2** and tape the wall surface above the line to keep it clean **3**. Apply thinset to the wall and floor using a ³/₁₆-in. by ³/₁₆-in. V-notched trowel **4** and embed the Kerdi Band with the flat side of the trowel **5**.

You can also use preformed corners and embed in the same way **6**. Peel off the blue painter's tape before the thinset cures **7**. If you wait, dried "crumbs" of thinset will fall onto your setting surface and make a mess.

Using the same notch trowel, "burn" or force the thinset into the DITRA where the sheets have met until the pockets are full **8**. Comb with the notch side and embed the Kerdi Band with the flat side of the trowel **9** .

1 Measure 2½ in. up the wall, in two places, for the Kerdi Band.

2 Snap a chalk line on the wall at the pencil marks to mark where the painter's tape will go.

3 Apply two rows of blue painter's tape to protect the wall.

4 Fill the cavities of the DITRA mat and then comb the thinset with a $3/16$-in. by $3/16$-in. V-notched trowel.

5 Use the flat end of the trowel to embed and flatten the Kerdi Band.

6 You can use pre-formed Kerdi corners or make your own. Embed them using the same process as before.

7 Peel the tape off the wall while the thinset is still wet.

8 Apply thinset to the DITRA and embed the Kerdi Band, using the flat side of the trowel.

9 Fill the cavities in the membrane at the seams with thinset. Roll out and embed the Kerdi Band.

PREPPING PLYWOOD SUBFLOORS

If the plywood subfloor that was underneath your carpet or finished flooring is still in good condition, you can use it again. But if you see evidence of damage (holes, water stain, rot) that affects the structural integrity of the wood, you need to replace the plywood in those areas. Use a circular saw to cut out a square or rectangle of plywood between two floor joists. Cut a new piece from the same thickness of plywood, and nail it down to the floor joists.

If your floor has a few dips or large gouges, it's a good idea to flatten them out by filling with a latex-modified thinset. Spread it across the defect area, then screed it off with a trowel or straightedge. If your floor is more seriously bumpy and uneven, you can flatten it using a self-leveling compound.

➡ **See "Applying Self-Leveling Compound," pp. 110-112.**

But before you can apply the compound over a plywood subfloor, you must nail down expanded metal lath, for reinforcement. Use caulking to fill any gaps between plywood sheets and to fill nail holes. Prime the surface, then nail or staple 2.5 galvanized expanded metal lath in place. Be sure to overlap the metal lath by 4 in. to 6 in. where sections meet. After the self-leveling compound has been applied and dried, the surface is ready for setting tile—no need for backerboard.

Staple-hammer overlapping **pieces of 2.5 metal lath over any wood subfloor before pouring a self-leveling compound.**

PREPPING VINYL FLOORING

You can lay tile over a vinyl floor, provided that there's no asbestos in the flooring and the vinyl is a single thickness and of the rigid type.

➡ **See "Removing Resilient Flooring," p. 103.**

To prepare a vinyl flooring for a layer of backerboard substrate, you'll need to sand the vinyl floor to rough it up. First, remove any vinyl cove baseboards by cutting the flooring with a razor knife, about 1½ in. from the wall, all the way around the room. Lift the vinyl flooring next to the cove with a prybar, then pull out the wood cove strip that is underneath. Now rough up the entire vinyl floor with an electric orbital sander fitted with 60-grit sandpaper ❶. Sanding gives the vinyl "tooth" for the thinset to adhere to. It also helps remove wax or dirt that may interfere with bonding. The surface is now ready for backerboard installation ❷.

➡ **See "Installing Backerboard on Floors," pp. 123-124.**

1 Sanding a vinyl floor with 60-grit sandpaper will give it the "tooth" it needs for adhering backerboard to it with thinset.

2 Comb the thinset and lay the backerboard over the sanded vinyl floor.

COUNTERTOP REPAIR AND PREP

1 Check the cabinet frames, front to back and side to side, for level.

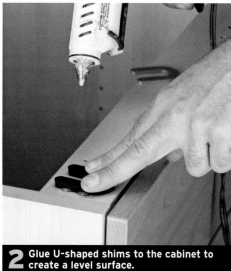

2 Glue U-shaped shims to the cabinet to create a level surface.

3 Screw the plywood down, avoiding the cabinet faces.

4 Protect the finished cabinet surfaces by taping rosin or kraft paper over them.

5 Roll two coats of waterproofing liquid on the countertop and backsplash areas.

After you've removed an old countertop from a cabinet, check to see if the rough top underneath is in good condition and level. If it is, consider yourself lucky and move ahead to waterproofing.

Otherwise, you need to fit a new plywood rough top. First, check the cabinet for level in all directions: right to left, and front to back **1**. Locate the highest spot, then work toward the lowest spot, adding U-shaped spacers every 6 in. with hot-melt glue **2**. Cut the new plywood to fit flush to the edges of the cabinet. If you need to use more than one piece, make sure that all plywood edges meet over a cabinet side or bulkhead. That way, each end can be screwed into something solid **3**. Make sure to screw through the spacers, not between them, to keep the plywood flat. Tape rosin paper to the face of all cabinets, to help protect them during subsequent operations **4**.

Because grout isn't waterproof and backerboard is only water resistant, it's important to apply a waterproof membrane.

The easiest way to do this is to roll on two coats of a liquid membrane product, such as RedGard, to the cabinet's rough top. First apply a coat over the entire surface of the plywood using a 3/4-in.-nap hand roller. Let the first coat cure and then add a second coat. If you're adding a backsplash to your countertop, apply two coats of the membrane to the wall behind the sink **5**.

BACKSPLASH WALL REPAIR AND PREP

1 Patch holes throughout the wall with a quick-drying compound.

2 Smooth large areas of applied compound with a broad knife.

C areful repair of holes and smoothing of bumps and valleys are important, because a flat surface will affect both the ease of installation and the final look of your tile. The smaller the tile you plan to install, the more defects show (every bump shows with small glass mosaic tiles). If you install larger rustic (irregular) tiles, wall irregularities are less noticeable.

To repair holes in your backsplash wall, use a fast-setting drywall or plaster repair mortar. Mix the powder with water (per the directions on the bag) and spread it with a putty knife ❶. Fill each hole, then lightly scrape it flat with the putty knife, switching to a wider knife if necessary ❷. If you find areas of drywall that flex excessively or are so soft that you can put your thumb through them, those sections will need to be replaced.

Cut out the bad section along the studs on both sides of the repair area ❸, then across the top and bottom. Remove the defective piece ❹ and clean up the edges of the hole alongside the studs. Measure the hole and cut a new piece of drywall to fit it ❺. If the new section is thinner than the existing wall thickness, add shim stock to the studs to make the patch flush with the wall. Screw the patch in place with drywall screws and ❻ tape the joints around the patch with drywall tape, to add additional strength ❼.

3 Cut out the damaged area of drywall with a razor knife.

4 Remove damaged section of wall by pulling it out carefully.

5 Measure the size of the opening for a new drywall patch.

6 Screw the new drywall patch firmly into the studs.

7 Tape the drywall joints with self-adhesive mesh tape.

FLATTENING THE WALL

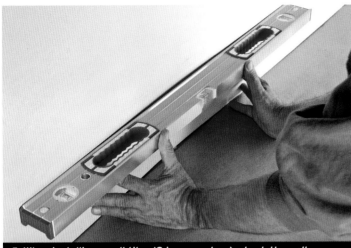

1 When installing small tiles (2 in. sq. or less), check the wall for bumps and valleys.

2 Fill the hollows in the wall surface with a quick-setting compound.

3 Screed off excess compound before it hardens, using a level.

4 Fill any low spots that are left with additional compound.

5 A nice flat wall, all ready for setting tile.

F or a good-looking tile installation, the backsplash wall should be flat, without big hills and valleys. Check for flatness by placing a straightedge or level across the area and marking the low areas ❶. Fill these areas by applying a quick-setting wall patch material ❷. We use 20-minute drywall patch for drywall areas, quick-setting plaster patch for plaster walls, and SpeedSet thinset for brick or concrete block walls. Use a straightedge or level to screed (skim) off excess material ❸. After letting the patch material firm up, apply more to any areas that are still low ❹. Screed off again and allow the surface to dry completely ❺. If your backsplash falls behind a sink area, you should now waterproof the wall by applying a liquid antifracture membrane, as described on pp. 72-74. Applying a membrane is also necessary if you plan to install glass tile.

CUTTING BACKERBOARD

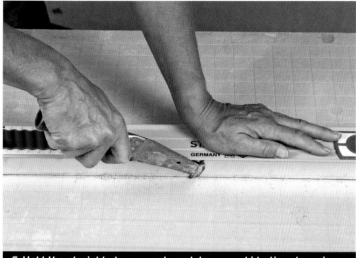

1 Hold the straightedge securely and drag a carbide-tipped scoring tool over the backerboard, to score it along the line of cut.

2 Position the backerboard with its scored line along the edge of a level or straightedge and apply downward pressure until it snaps.

3 Use a compass or round object to mark out circular cutouts for fixtures.

4 Dry-fit the cut backerboard piece and mark any areas that need to be trimmed.

5 Trim backerboard with tile nippers and recheck the fit.

One of the last steps in preparing a wood floor, countertop, or wall surface for tiling is to install backerboard. Concrete backerboard creates a solid, durable substrate for tile work to be set on top of. It's affordable, easy to cut, and helps make these installations structurally sound and long lasting. Backerboard installation is a four-step process: Measure and cut the board to size, bond it to the surface, fasten it with nails or screws, and then tape the joints. Start by

measuring the area that'll be tiled and calculate the number of sheets of backerboard to buy. Then figure the size and shape of each piece you'll need to cut.

You can cut backerboard by hand using a scoring tool or with the use of power tools. If you cut by hand, mark your cut and use a scoring tool along a straightedge to score the sheet ❶. Match up the backerboard's scored edge with one edge of the straightedge and apply pressure downward,

breaking off the scored board ❷. For more complicated cuts, like L-shaped cuts around a cabinet or a circle for a toilet flange ❸ or heating vent, use an angle grinder or jigsaw. Because these tools generate lots of dust, cut outdoors whenever possible and definitely wear a dust mask, goggles, and hearing protectors. Test-fit your piece ❹ and trim with tile nippers as necessary ❺. Always do this before spreading thinset to avoid a real mess.

INSTALLING BACKERBOARD ON FLOORS

1 Use the short end of a trowel to spread thinset in cramped areas, such as around this toilet flange.

2 Lower the backerboard into place over the toilet flange, working its corner under the cabinet.

3 Nail backerboard into place following the nail pattern on the board or every 6 in. in each direction.

4 In cramped areas, like under cabinet toekicks, use the side of the hammer head to bang nails into place.

After cutting the backerboard to size, spread latex-modified thinset on top of the wood subfloor (or prepared vinyl floor) with a ¼-in. by ¼-in. notched trowel **1**. Carefully lower the backerboard onto the thinset and press in place **2**. Use either nails or screws to fasten the sheet to the wood floor, making sure you use enough nails (see the specifications for the backerboard). Some sheets have a nailing pattern embossed on the surface for you to follow **3**. If you are working under a toekick, use the side of the hammer to drive nails **4**. >> >> >>

INSTALLING BACKERBOARD ON FLOORS (CONTINUED)

Omitting nails here can lead to a loose substrate, and problems with the tile later on. Continue adding sheets, as necessary, until the entire floor is covered ❺. Then tape every joint with fiberglass tape ❻ and cover with a thin layer of thinset, using the flat side of the trowel to embed it fully ❼.

TRADE SECRET
Splitting a full-size sheet of backerboard in two makes it easier to carry and install and will help you avoid dinging cabinets and walls as you work.

5 Continue spreading thinset and applying backerboard over the rest of the floor, nailing each piece into place.

6 Tape every backerboard seam with self-adhesive mesh tape.

7 Cover the mesh seams with a thin coat of thinset, to hold the mesh firmly in place.

INSTALLING BACKERBOARD ON COUNTERTOPS

Before installing backerboard on a countertop, you first need to determine how thick it must be to accommodate the trim tiles you plan to use on the front edge of your counter. The backerboard must support the trim so that its bottom edge doesn't interfere with the cabinet drawers, doors, or appliances below it. To figure the correct height, take a trim tile and a field tile and hold them at the counter's edge ❶. Measure the distance between the bottom of the field tile and the plywood rough top. This dimension equals the total backerboard thickness you'll need. Because backerboard comes only in 1/4-in. and 1/2-in. thicknesses, you may need to install two (or more) layers to get the correct thickness.

Cut the backerboard to match the dimensions of the cabinet top, but less 1/8 in. wherever it butts against a wall (to allow for bumps and bows in the wall).

➡ See "Cutting Backerboard," p. 122.

The backerboard should fit flush with the cabinet's finished ends and front edge. Use a 1/4-in. by 1/4-in. notched trowel to spread latex-modified thinset onto the waterproofed plywood rough top ❷. Lay the backerboard on the thinset, then nail it down with 1 1/2-in.-ring shank nails. Follow the nailing pattern printed on the board (typically, every 6 in. across the board) ❸. If a second layer of backerboard is needed, cut these pieces so that their ends will be staggered relative to the board underneath (for better strength). Use thinset to bond the second layer to the first, and nail it down as before.

Now measure for the strips of backerboard that'll trim the counter edges. Place your edge trim in place and measure its height from the top of the backerboard surface to the bottom of the trim. The edge piece should not be so wide as to extend beyond the bottom of the trim tile. Cut these narrow pieces with care, then back-butter them with thinset ❹ and nail them in place ❺. Finally, cover all seams and edges with fiberglass tape ❻.

1 Backerboard should be high enough for trim to clear doors and drawers.

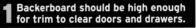

2 Apply a coat of thinset with a 1/4-in. by 1/4-in. notched trowel.

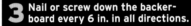

3 Nail or screw down the backerboard every 6 in. in all directions.

4 Back-butter the front edge piece of backerboard with thinset.

5 Nail the front edge piece into the plywood rough top.

6 Apply fiberglass tape to the joint between the top and the front edge.

CUTTING OUT FOR A SINK

1 To center the sink, first draw the cabinet's centerline onto the rough top.

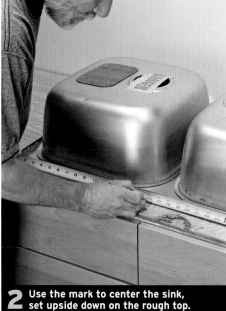

2 Use the mark to center the sink, set upside down on the rough top.

3 Position the sink, leaving at least 2 in. for the plumbing at the back.

4 Using the sink as a template, draw an outline on the rough top.

5 Use a jigsaw to cut ½ in. inside the sink outline.

6 Cut well inside the sink outline, leaving a lip for the rim of the sink.

I f your countertop has a sink in it, you'll need to cut a hole in the plywood rough top before installing the backerboard.

Start by finding the center point of your sink cabinet and aligning your framing square with it. Mark a centerline along the square all the way up the plywood to the wall **1**. Now place your sink (or paper sink template) on the counter and center it on your centerline **2**. Measure the distance between the sink and the front of the cabinet in several places, to make sure they are parallel **3**. (If you have an oval sink, the template provided will have front and back centerlines to help with alignment.) After marking the outline of the sink **4**, use a jigsaw to make a cut space ½ in. *inside* the marked outline **5**. If you cut on your line, the sink will fall through, and nobody wants to do dishes on the floor **6**!

BACKERBOARD FOR AN OVERMOUNT SINK

Backerboard installation depends on the kind of sink you plan to use: stainless steel or cast iron, and overmount or undermount. An overmount sink has a rim that sits atop the counter tile and is relatively easy to install and easy to replace if it becomes chipped or damaged. An undermount sink sits underneath the tile surface and has a recessed design that makes countertop clean-ups easier but is more complicated to install.

To install an overmount sink (stainless steel or cast iron), size and cut a piece of backerboard to fit atop the plywood, as described on p. 126. Mark the sink cutout by setting the backerboard on top of the plywood and then climbing underneath to mark the outline of the sink opening ❶. Don your safety apparel and cut along the line with a jigsaw or a small angle grinder ❷. Now install the backerboard atop the plywood with thinset, nail it in place, and tape all seams between the backerboard sheets ❸. If you need another layer of backerboard to accommodate your edge trim, cut out the additional pieces and set them in place with thinset ❹. Mount the sink after the tile is set and grouted.

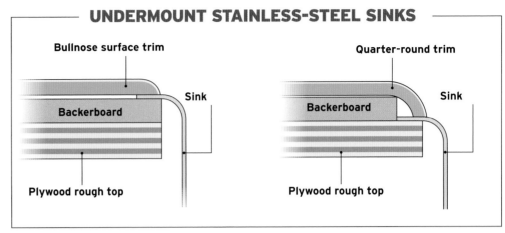

UNDERMOUNT STAINLESS-STEEL SINKS

Bullnose surface trim

Sink

Backerboard

Plywood rough top

Quarter-round trim

Sink

Backerboard

Plywood rough top

1 Reach under the countertop to mark the backerboard for a sink cutout.

2 Support the narrow front and back edges of the backerboard when cutting.

3 If your backerboard splits, tape the crack with self-adhesive mesh tape.

4 Another layer may be needed to accommodate wide front edge trim.

UNDERMOUNT SINK WITH QUARTER-ROUND TRIM

Installing a stainless-steel sink with quarter-round trim takes two steps. To accommodate a typical ½-in.-radius quarter-round, the sink must sit below the top of the backerboard by ½ in. (always check your particular quarter-round as trim can vary in size). This requires two layers of backerboard: The sink sits on the lower layer of backerboard and a second layer of ½-in. backerboard adds the correct thickness, allowing the lower edge of the quarter-round to bear against the sink rim.

→ **See the drawing "Cast-Iron Sinks" on the facing page.**

The first backerboard layer is cut out for the sink and bonded to the plywood.

→ **See "Cutting Out for a Sink," p. 126 and "Backerboard for an Overmount Sink," p. 127.**

A second backerboard layer is then sized and cut to fit the countertop. The sink cutout in this layer must cut slightly larger to allow for the placement of the quarter-round: Start by measuring the distance from the front edge of the countertop to the inside of the sink cutout in the first backerboard layer ❶. Now set the new backerboard in position on the countertop and lay the sink on it upside down. Set the sink back from the front edge of the backerboard by the dimension obtained earlier ❷, measuring from the inside metal frame of the sink, not its outer rim. Draw a line around the sink's rim

1 Measure from the front edge of the countertop to the inside edge of the sink opening.

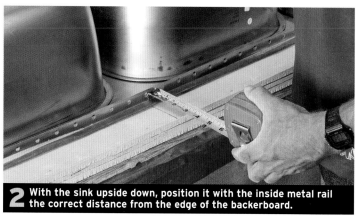

2 With the sink upside down, position it with the inside metal rail the correct distance from the edge of the backerboard.

UNDERMOUNT SINK WITH BULLNOSE TRIM

Installing an undermount stainless-steel sink is easy if you will surround it with bullnose trim. Simply cut and install a layer of backerboard as described for an overmount sink, on p. 113. Place the sink into the cutout directly atop the backerboard and fasten it in place. Because stainless-steel sinks have a tendency to flex and not lay completely flat, place a screw in each corner, at the outside edge of the rim ❶. Use a block of wood to prevent the screwdriver tip from accidentally skittering and marring the sink. When you install tile on the countertop, the bullnose trim will overlay the rim of the sink ❷.

1 Drive screws at the corners of a stainless-steel sink to hold the sink flat.

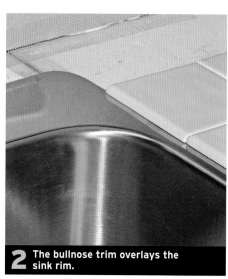

2 The bullnose trim overlays the sink rim.

and make your cutout along this line ❸. Get a helping hand to set the piece in place, so as not to break the narrow strips around the sink cutout. Carefully lift and carry the top piece of backerboard in to dry-fit it in place ❹. Place your sink into the cutout, trowel with thinset, and then fasten the top piece of backerboard with nails or screws and tape any seams. To protect the sink, place a piece of cardboard over the top before doing any tile work. This is your shield against dropped tools and dripped thinset when setting tile.

3 Trace around the perimeter of the sink to mark the cutout.

4 Carefully fit the backerboard in place.

CAST-IRON SINKS

Cast-iron sinks are durable and long lasting and come in enameled hues that can add color to your countertop. Cast-iron sinks are undermounted in a similar fashion to stainless-steel sinks, and the installation depends on whether you use bullnose or quarter-round trim.

To install a typical cast-iron sink with a $1/2$-in.-thick rim on a counter with bullnose trim, set the sink on the plywood rough top and install $1/2$-in. backerboard around it. Use the sink as a template and cut the hole in the backerboard about $1/8$ in. larger. Install the tile, finishing around the sink with the bullnose trim tiles.

If you prefer the look of a cast-iron sink trimmed with quarter-round tiles, install a layer of $1/2$-in. backerboard, then add another sheet of $1/2$-in. backerboard over it to create space for the quarter-round trim. Both sheets should be cut slightly larger than the outside edge of the sink.

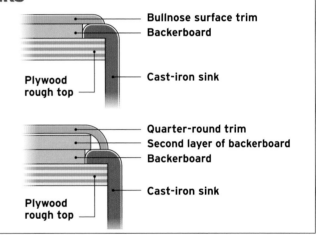

Bullnose surface trim
Backerboard
Plywood rough top
Cast-iron sink

Quarter-round trim
Second layer of backerboard
Backerboard
Plywood rough top
Cast-iron sink

BACKERBOARD ON A BACKSPLASH

Tile for a backsplash can be installed directly on drywall that's been properly prepared (see pp. 120–121). But for a backsplash trimmed with quarter-rounds, you must install backerboard under the tile to provide the depth needed for the trim. Regular $1/2$-in. backerboard is the right thickness to use with most quarter-round trim (measure your trim just to be sure). Cut the backerboard the same size as the over-all dimension of the backsplash. Using a stud finder, mark each stud position on the wall. Then, with a notched trowel, back-butter the backerboard with thinset ❶. Secure the backerboard to the wall with 2-in. nails or screws, making sure you hit the studs. (If the edge of the board does not fall on a stud, use thinset to hold it in place. Place a weight against the board to keep it in firm contact with the wall as the thinset dries.) Tape all joints with mesh tape ❷.

1 Apply modified thinset to the rear of a backerboard strip.

2 After nailing the backerboard in place, tape the joint.

METHODS OF PLANNING LAYOUT

A good layout plans the locations of cut tiles carefully so that the tile's factory edges (rather than cut edges) show in prominent locations and there are no out-of-place-looking narrow cut tiles.

By exploring various layout options before setting the first tile, you can make sure tiles are arranged symmetrically around sinks, cooktops, and cabinetry, and prevent an awkward misalignment between rows of tile and trim.

Depending on the size of your tile job and your working preferences, there are several methods for creating a layout plan.

Drawing on graph paper is an easy way to do a scale drawing of a small tile layout, such as a countertop, bathroom floor, or entryway (make 1/4 in.= 1 ft.). Do your drawing in pencil, so you can try out different ideas. Once you've worked out cut tile loca-

tions, decorative tile placement, and so on, you'll end up with a drawing you can refer to while setting tile.

For smaller jobs, like countertops and bathroom floors, you can lay out the tiles on a work surface.

For larger jobs, it's easier to do the trial layout on the floor, where you have plenty of room to work. Lay out a row or two, using spacers between tiles if necessary, and check the dimensions to determine where the cut tiles will be. Although time-consuming, this method provides a preview of exactly how a tile installation will look.

For complex situations, such as multi-room tile floors, a CAD (computer-aided design) program provides great assistance and flexibility with tile layout. Simple CAD programs are affordable and provide all the features and options you'll need to try

Dry-lay the tile on your work surface to check spacing and cuts.

out different arrays (tiles laid square or diagonally), centering options, and border or trim configurations without having to erase a single line or lift a single tile. Print out a copy of your plan and you're ready to tile.

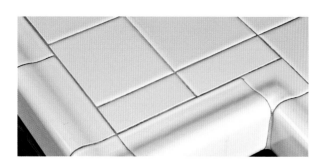

Narrow cut tiles aren't a first choice, but sometimes they allow the rest of the countertop to lay out beautifully.

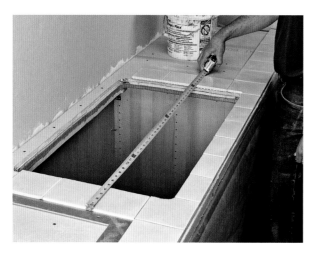

Plan your layout carefully around sinks and other focal points to keep cut tiles symmetrical.

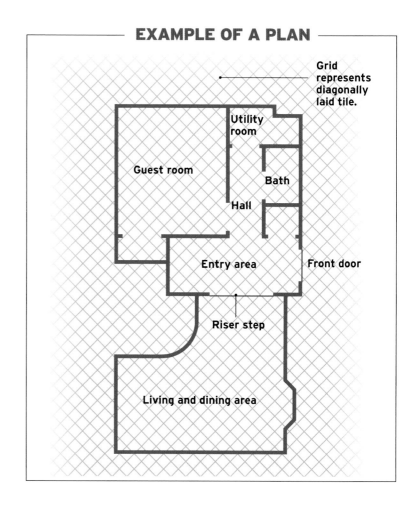

EXAMPLE OF A PLAN

Grid represents diagonally laid tile.

Utility room

Guest room

Bath

Hall

Entry area

Front door

Riser step

Living and dining area

PLANNING COUNTERTOP LAYOUT

A A top bullnose should be set before the cut face tiles are placed.

B Lay out and set your field tiles first when using a bullnose as a fascia piece.

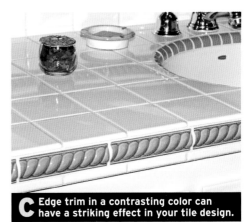

C Edge trim in a contrasting color can have a striking effect in your tile design.

D When the front edge trim is a different size from the field tile, setting it on the face of the countertop is the best option.

E Corners may require some cutting so the edge trim lines up with the field tile.

No matter what the shape of your counter, a good looking tile layout starts with a row of full tiles along the front top edge of the countertop. This leaves any cut tiles at the back, where the counter meets the wall or backsplash. But before you begin your layout, you must determine and mark out exactly where that first row of tile will start relative to the counter's front edge. This is affected by the kind of edge trim you've chosen and the way you will install it. Edge trim commonly comes in two styles: surface bullnose and V-cap.

➡ See "Trim," pp. 26–27.

Surface bullnose either can be set on top of the counter, overlapping edge trim cut from field tiles **A**, or can be cut and set vertically on the edge of the counter **B**.

Setting the bullnose on the top is the easier of the two arrangements, especially if the trim tiles are the exact same size as the field tiles. Setting the bullnose on the top also allows you to use decorative border tiles for the front edge fascia **C**. If your design calls for using contrasting-color bullnose trim on the counter's front edge, you'll want to set the bullnose vertically for a stronger visual impact **D**. Setting bullnose vertically is also a good trim choice for L- or U-shaped counters, when the field tile is a different size than the trim. You lay out and center the trim, allowing for good-size cuts at the inside and outside corners. For example, on the counter in photo **E**, the surface bullnose edge trim is larger than the field tile and the two will never line up.

LAYING OUT EDGES

V-cap is not only decorative but also can be practical. Many styles of this trim have a raised lip that prevents rounded objects from rolling off, great for a kitchen counter or bathroom vanity. V-cap is set on the edge of the counter with its rear edge flush with the surface of the field tile. Because V-cap is fixed in height, the counter's rough top and substrate must be the right thickness to accommodate it.

> **See "Installing Backerboard on Countertops," p. 125.**

Determine exactly where, relative to the edge of the counter substrate, the first row of tiles will start, then draw a layout line to guide the installation.

Use a level or straightedge to put a pencil mark along the back edge of the bullnose. To find where to draw the first-row layout line for V-cap (or edge-laid bullnose trim), hold a field tile and edge piece in place on the counter edge and make a pencil mark at the back edge of the field tile ❶. Use a tile spacer (if necessary) to leave room for the grout joint. Mark this distance at both ends of the counter, then join the lines with a straightedge ❷. It's a good idea to also measure the distance between this layout line and the back of the countertop, to see if they are parallel. If they are not, you'll need to take this into account when you install the tile.

1 To obtain the layout line for your field tiles, hold a V-cap and field tile in place, then make a pencil line behind the back edge of the field tile. Repeat on the other side of the counter.

2 Your level or straightedge will help you to connect the marks so you can make a line all the way down the countertop for the field tiles.

In the case of top-mounted bullnose,

the first row will actually be bullnose tile. To mark the layout line, set the bullnose and edge trim in place so that the front edge of the bullnose is flush with the surface of the trim. Check that the bullnose provides enough overhang to allow for the thickness of the edge piece along with some thinset behind it.

LAYING OUT A SINK COUNTER

If only one end of the countertop butts up against a wall, the easiest layout is to start laying a full tile at the corner of the open end of the counter, and set full tiles toward the wall. If any cut pieces are needed, they will be closest to the wall, where they will show the least. A row of full tiles also starts at the front edge of the counter, so that cut tiles are at the backsplash.

The best-looking solution for a small counter with open ends on both sides is to lay the tiles symmetrically, relative to the centerline of the cabinet. This requires cut field tiles at both ends of the counter as well as along the back. If the tiles fall so that these cut pieces are narrower than half a tile, an optional layout is to start with full tiles at the ends of the counter, and cut the row of tiles in the center to fit. These strategies will also work for rectangular counters that are surrounded by walls on three sides as well as for freestanding counters, such as kitchen islands.

A symmetrical, centered tile layout is also favorable for countertops that house sinks or appliances, such as cooktops and grills. Because the eye is drawn to these features, it's important that the tile surrounding them is even on both sides. For example, to lay out tile for a simple rectangular kitchen sink counter, start by drawing a pencil line on the substrate that's centered on the middle of the sink cutout and perpendicular to the long edge of the counter. Now try two different layouts by placing a row of tiles along the counter's edge starting at the centerline mark. For the first, lay the first tile with its edge flush to the centerline (offset slightly to account for the grout joint) **A**. For the second, lay the first tile so that its center aligns with the centerline **B**. Choose the layout that leaves the widest row of cut tiles on each side of the sink. For the sink counter shown in this example, the first option (grout joint on the centerline) is more favorable **C**. Centering your tile layout may also be desirable if there's a window, cabinet, or other prominent feature above the countertop. Follow the same procedure as for centering tile on a sink. Before finalizing the layout, it's prudent to lay tiles all the way down the length of the countertop, to check the size of the cut pieces needed at both ends.

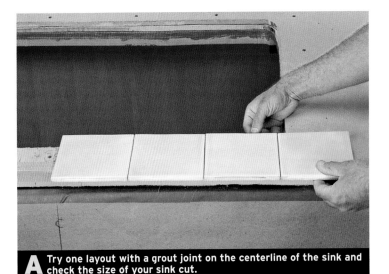

A Try one layout with a grout joint on the centerline of the sink and check the size of your sink cut.

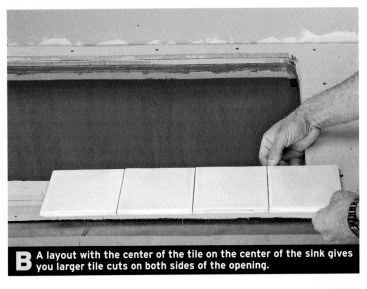

B A layout with the center of the tile on the center of the sink gives you larger tile cuts on both sides of the opening.

C The winning layout in this case was to place the joint in the center, yielding good-size cuts on both sides of the sink.

L- AND U-SHAPED COUNTERS

As the shape of a countertop becomes more complex, so does the tile layout. For example, consider the L-shaped counter with sink, shown in the top drawing at right. Centering the tile relative to the sink, as described on p. 135, results in a narrow row of field tiles along the front edge of the adjacent counter—not a desirable layout. A more favorable alternative is to use a full-size tile at the inside corner of the L, and lay a row of full-size tiles along both counter edges. This creates a nonsymmetrical spacing of tiles at the sides of the sink, but the overall look of the countertop is better.

Things can get even more complicated with U-shaped countertops, especially when one or more legs of the counter house a sink and/or appliances. On the counter arrangement shown in the bottom drawing at right, centering tiles relative to the cooktop results in narrow field tiles at the front edges of the two parallel counters. The best compromise in this case is to add a cut tile near the center of the cooktop (the red tile in the drawing). Pro tilers call this a "Dutchman". This layout allows you to set full-size tiles on all counter edges. In any case, it's best to dry-lay every possibility because each L- and U-shaped counter configuration is different and there is no one correct layout; it is your preference.

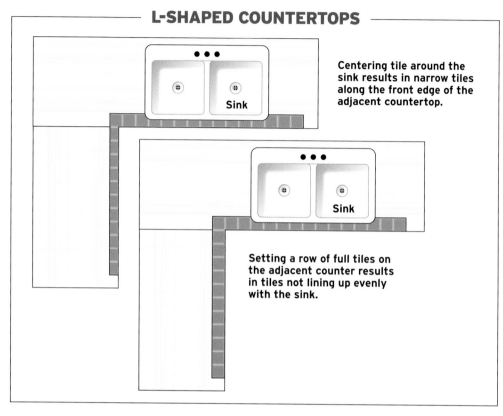

L-SHAPED COUNTERTOPS

Centering tile around the sink results in narrow tiles along the front edge of the adjacent countertop.

Setting a row of full tiles on the adjacent counter results in tiles not lining up evenly with the sink.

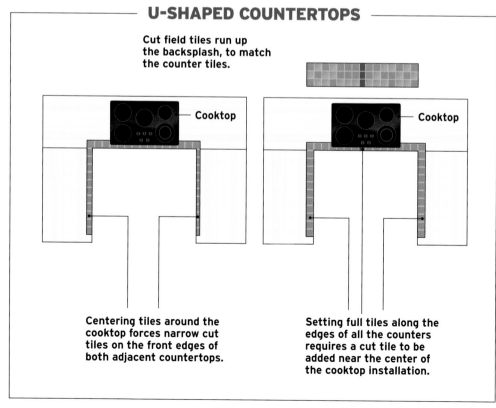

U-SHAPED COUNTERTOPS

Cut field tiles run up the backsplash, to match the counter tiles.

Centering tiles around the cooktop forces narrow cut tiles on the front edges of both adjacent countertops.

Setting full tiles along the edges of all the counters requires a cut tile to be added near the center of the cooktop installation.

BACKSPLASH LAYOUT

When the backsplash and field tiles are the same size, just line up the grout joints.

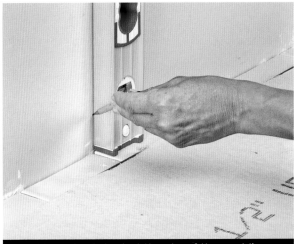

1 Hold your level plumb at the edge of the grout line and draw a line all the way up the wall.

Once you've determined your countertop layout, the backsplash should follow those field tiles up the wall. Simply line up the tiles on the splash with the tiles on the countertop, making sure the grout joints match up. But what if your backsplash tile isn't the same size as your countertop tile or you plan to set the splash tiles diagonally? In this case, center the tile relative to the overall length of the counter.

➤ See "Laying Out a Sink Counter," p. 135.

Start by marking the center point of the counter, then draw a vertical line up the wall, using a level to ensure that it's plumb ❶. You'll set your tile starting at this line and working out toward the ends. Even if your tile is the same size as the countertop tile and lines up with it, the trim you use at the finished edges of your backsplash may not be the same size. In such a case, use this same centering technique to set the trim tiles.

You also need to plan where your backsplash tiles will end at the ends of the countertop. Depending on how your countertop is situated, you may end the splash flush with the end of the countertop or with the edge of upper cabinets, or you can run it so it butts up against an adjacent wall, door, window frame, or other element. In this example, we chose to end the tiles flush with the upper cabinet on the right side and lined up the lower cabinet on the left. Ultimately, choose the alignment that looks best in your particular situation.

Electrical boxes on a full-height backsplash will probably need some cut outs. Kitchens and bathrooms usually have electrical outlets and switches located several inches above counter level. There are two ways to plan your backsplash to accommodate this: Make a short splash that ends below the outlets or make a tall splash and cut the tiles to fit around outlets. The latter choice requires a bit more work, but a tall backsplash provides more protection for the wall, important in areas behind sinks and cooktops ❷. The finished backsplash complements the cabinets and fits nicely into the space ❸.

2 Plan ahead for electrical boxes so that they don't fall within decorative tiles.

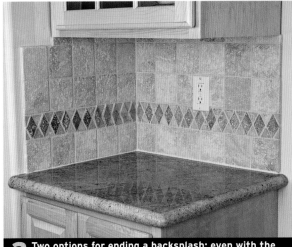

3 Two options for ending a backsplash: even with the upper cabinet or even with the edge of the countertop.

FLOOR LAYOUT

Starting with a full tile at a doorway leads you into the room and prevents the distraction of small cut tiles at this very visible location.

Although a floor presents a much larger surface to tile than a counter or backsplash, the basic tenets of layout are the same: Strive for a balanced, clean look, with full tiles in prominent locations and cut tiles falling where they won't draw attention. The steps to create a layout are a bit different whether you're tiling a room with one or two doorways or a more complicated space with hallways, steps, and other transitions. Irregular and stone tile floors also demand their own layout considerations.

Single-doorway floor

Tile layout in a simple square or rectangular room with a single doorway is quite straight-forward. The layout looks best with a full tile starting at the doorway (cut tiles at the doorway

can be distracting). Subsequent rows of full tiles line up from the doorway, leaving any cut tiles at the opposite side of the room where they're less noticeable and may be covered by furnishings or cabinets.

Start your layout by snapping a chalkline across the doorway (1), midway underneath the closed door. Snap a second line perpendicular to the first (2), centered in the jamb. Now dry-lay a row of tiles along the edge of the perpendicular line (with spacers, as necessary) from the first line to the opposite wall. Mark the far edge of the last full tile near the wall, then snap a third line perpendicular to the second line at this mark (3), as shown in the top drawing at right.

Now dry-lay tiles along the third line, to preview the size of

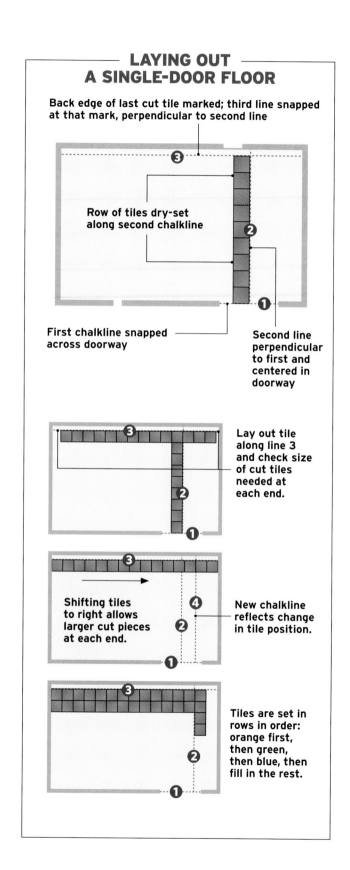

LAYING OUT A SINGLE-DOOR FLOOR

Back edge of last cut tile marked; third line snapped at that mark, perpendicular to second line

Row of tiles dry-set along second chalkline

First chalkline snapped across doorway

Second line perpendicular to first and centered in doorway

Lay out tile along line 3 and check size of cut tiles needed at each end.

Shifting tiles to right allows larger cut pieces at each end.

New chalkline reflects change in tile position.

Tiles are set in rows in order: orange first, then green, then blue, then fill in the rest.

To start a diagonal layout, begin with a half tile at the doorway.

 WHAT CAN GO WRONG
Don't worry if walls, cabinets, tub enclosures, and so on, aren't square to your floor layout lines. Simply set the closest row of tile that's aligned with your layout, then cut tiles at the necessary taper to fit.

cut tiles at the ends. If one of the cuts is very small and very visible, you can shift the tiles toward one side of the room or the other; just remember that this affects the tile layout across the doorway. If you do shift tiles, you'll need to mark the new grout joint position and snap a fourth line parallel to line 2 (4). When you're ready to lay tile, you'll set tile in the order shown in the bottom drawing on the facing page, using the layout lines to keep the tile rows straight and true.

Dual-doorway floor

The best-looking tile layout in a room with two entrances is with full tiles starting at both doorways. The layout is very similar to a single-door-room layout:

After snapping chalklines across the thresholds of both doors (1, 2), snap a line perpendicular to the room's primary entrance (3); then lay a row of tile along the edge of that line, from that doorway to the opposite wall.

Now choose a grout joint that lines up somewhere in the middle of the room's secondary entrance, mark its position, and snap another perpendicular line (4), as shown in the drawing at right. Remove the first row of tiles, dry-lay tiles along the fourth line, and then shift the tile position back and forth until you have a full tile at the secondary entrance. Finally, strike another line (5) parallel to 3, so that tiles will line up in both doorways.

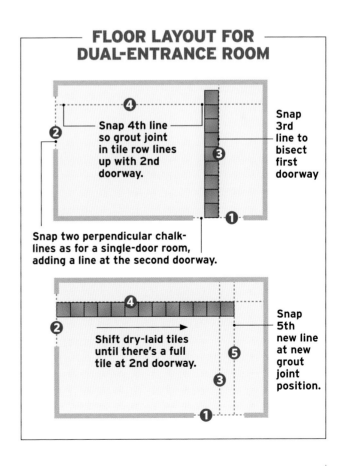

FLOOR LAYOUT FOR DUAL-ENTRANCE ROOM

Snap 4th line so grout joint in tile row lines up with 2nd doorway.

Snap 3rd line to bisect first doorway

Snap two perpendicular chalklines as for a single-door room, adding a line at the second doorway.

Shift dry-laid tiles until there's a full tile at 2nd doorway.

Snap 5th new line at new grout joint position.

COMPLEX FLOORS

Tile layout on an irregular-shaped floor or one that continues through a number of rooms and hallways becomes a bit more complicated. When faced with a complex diagonally set tile floor (for a home with an entry, riser step down to a living and dining room, and a hallway leading into a bathroom and guest room), we used a CAD program to explore different layout schemes.

➤ **See the drawing "Example of a Plan," p. 132.**

This layout starts with full tiles on the entry area riser (the focal point of the space) leading into the living/dining space ❶. Fortunately, the width of the entry allowed full, uncut diagonal tiles at both sides. Lengthwise, we decided it was important to have tiles centered in the main hallway off the entry, but that required cut tiles at the doorways at both ends of the entry (complex layouts always require compromises).

Our first step was to snap a chalkline just back from the riser step, as a point of reference to lay the tile. After sweeping and washing the floor, we measured and confirmed that the entry wall was parallel to the riser ❷. Next, we measured and marked the position of the bullnose tile used at the edge of the riser (this narrow trim helps differentiate the edge of the riser, preventing tripping accidents) ❸. We made two marks the same distance from the wall and snapped our chalkline where the first row of full tiles would start at the back edge of the bullnose ❹. Next, we used a 3-4-5 triangle to create a line perpendicular to the line along the riser ❺. Then we measured and snapped another line down the center of

>> >> >>

1 A full tile on a diagonal layout means that you'll start with full tiles flanked by diagonal half tiles.

2 Measure each side of the entryway to see if the far wall is parallel to the step.

3 Mock up the bullnose and riser tile to mark their position on the stair.

4 Snap a red chalk line between the marks to create a reference line for the bullnose tile and a starting point for the field tile.

5 This alternately colored perpendicular chalkline provides a square reference mark.

KEEPING IT SQUARE WITH A 3-4-5 TRIANGLE

If you've ever wondered if you'd find a real-world application for the theorems and formulas you learned in high-school geometry, here's a good one for you: The Pythagorean theorem states that any triangle with sides that are 3 units, 4 units, and 5 units long will form a right angle between the two shorter sides.

By laying out a large 3-4-5 triangle with a tape measure (work in feet, yards, or meters—it doesn't matter), you can lay out lines that are perfectly square to one another or check the alignment of tiles laid diagonally across a large room. This method is much more versatile and accurate than checking with even the largest carpenter's framing square.

COMPLEX FLOORS (CONTINUED)

6 Measure to the center of the hallway and determine the difference between this measurement and the blue reference line.

7 Using your original chalk color, snap a line parallel to the blue reference line to mark the center of the hallway.

8 Use the red layout lines to set the tiles straight and perpendicular to each other. Line up the points of the tiles on the lines.

9 Line up a 4-ft. level with the points of the set tiles. Use a small level to transfer that line to the lower area.

the hallway **6**, **7**. By placing the diagonal points of each tile on this line, we could set the tiles in a straight, even row down the hallway. We used these layout lines to set tile in the entry and hallway **8**. Then we used the already set tiles to extend the diagonal layout into the other rooms. Using a 4-ft. level as a straightedge, we lined it up with the points of the upper room tiles. A small level allowed us to accurately transfer that mark to the parallel line in the lower area **9** so we could snap a line perpendicular to that mark.

LAYOUT FOR IRREGULAR TILES

Handmade terra-cotta pavers and some kinds of stone tiles are not consistent in size. If you try to lay out a floor for these tiles using the methods previously described, you'll end up with uneven rows and higgly-piggly-set tiles. To solve this problem, we set irregular tiles by snapping a grid of chalklines all the way across the floor. Each grid square is sized to hold nine full tiles ❶. The idea is that individual tiles may be adjusted relative to each other within the grid, to even out the spaces between them for a pleasing overall effect ❷. To determine the grid size, take three tiles at random and lay them on the floor. Space the tiles as per your chosen grout joint, remembering that irregular tiles need larger grout lines to compensate for their differences. The length of this tile layout from end to end, plus one grout joint, equals the size of the tile grid ❸. Add this grid to your tile layout plan or drawing to map out the position of the individual grids on the floor. Room dimensions will likely require some partial grids with cut tiles, so adjust the layout accordingly. Snap the grid of chalklines on the floor, using 3-4-5 triangles to keep the lines square.

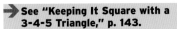

➤ See "Keeping It Square with a 3-4-5 Triangle," p. 143.

1 Setting irregular tiles is easiest when you use a grid of nine tiles.

2 By moving the tiles within each grid, you will achieve a more even look with irregular tiles.

3 Measure three tiles set in a row. The grid will be the size of the three tiles plus the width of one additional grout joint.

STONE TILE LAYOUT

Because each tile cut from natural stone is unique, your layout should best reflect the tile's individual patterns and color variations. The arrangement of veining and color patterns and interesting features, such as fossils or crystals, all have a profound effect on the look of your final installation.

Unpack all the boxes of stone tiles and examine their colors and features. Lay out the tiles before you begin setting to choose the pattern that pleases you most. If the tiles have prominent vein patterns, you might want to lay them out so that they all flow in the same direction **A** or you may prefer to alternate the way the veins run, to create a pattern of alternating horizontal and vertical lines **B**. Alternatively, you may like the look of a random arrangement even better **C**. If there are strong color variations between tiles, you'll want to mix the tiles up, so that the overall color of the installation is more even. After laying the tiles out and finalizing your pattern (or random arrangement), tag the individual tiles by sticking on a piece of tape, then labeling each one with a row and column number and an arrow that shows its orientation. The labeling lets you repeat your desired pattern when you set the tiles.

A Trying to match swirls or veins can achieve a look that emulates a solid sheet of stone.

B A complex pattern of alternating veins and swirls is busier but may be more interesting.

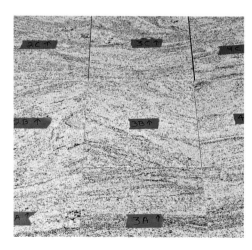

When you have chosen the pattern for your stone floor, label and mark each one with letters and numbers for rows and columns and add an orientation direction.

C A random pattern works best when there is significant variation in color or pattern, minimizing differences.

Tiles set on the diagonal in a classic checkerboard pattern open up this small bathroom.

The solid color of the wall in this bath contrasts with the dark and light pattern on the floor.

This glazed stoneware tile set in a random pattern adds just the right touch to a country kitchen.

Try a different approach

A floor gives you a large canvas for your designs. Don't be afraid to mix colors and shapes to get the look you want. Remember that the room will look bigger or smaller depending on the layout of the tile. A small room or hallway can look larger if the tiles are set on the diagonal. In a very small space, a busy pattern can be overwhelming; a room with a simple pattern on the wall can handle a more complex floor pattern.

TILING AN ENTRY AREA

Large diagonally set porcelain tiles create a beautiful, durable floor that covers this home's entry area, hallway, and living/dining areas.

1 A long chalkline provides a reference line for setting the first row of entry tiles and the bullnose trim to be set on the edge of the step.

W hether you are tiling a simple rectangular room with a single doorway, or a large, multilevel space with several doors and halls branching off of it, most of the basic tile-laying procedures you need to follow are very much the same. The large porcelain (18 in. sq.) tiles on this floor were laid in several stages: first, the entry area; then the main floor; next, the step and riser; and, finally, the cut tiles around the perimeter. Before tile setting started, we prepared the substrate (a concrete slab).

➡ **See "Prepping Concrete Floors," p. 109.**

We also planned the tile layout of the entire space, designed to yield a clean design, with the diagonally set tiles flowing across the entry area and into the living room.

➡ **See "Complex Floors," pp. 142-144.**

For this project, begin by snapping a chalkline to mark where the first row of tile is set at the edge of the steps ❶, and a perpendicular line to mark the center of the layout ❷. Then, spread and comb the area with thinset ❸.

➡ **See "Spreading Thinset," pp. 82-83.**

The first tile, cut in half diagonally, is set where the two chalklines intersect, with its apex and cut edge lined up with the lines ❹. Add tile spacers at the corners of the first tile, then set the next tile against it ❺. Continue to spread thinset and set subsequent tiles, making sure that the long edges of diagonal half tiles are butted up to the chalkline ❻.

2 A chalkline snapped down the center of the hallway marks the center of the tile pattern in the entry area.

3 Thinset is spread and combed in the area where the first tile is to be set, at the intersection of the chalklines.

4 The first half tile begins the diagonal layout pattern that will run across the entire floor.

5 Subsequent tiles are set aligned to the first tile, with spacers between them to maintain even grout joints.

SETTING LARGE TILES

Big tiles—15 in. x 15 in. and larger—and stone tiles weigh substantially more than basic 12-in.-sq. floor tiles. There are two things you can do to make your life easier when setting them: Use large-format thinset and a suction lifter. Large-format thinset has larger sand grains and won't sag under the weight of big tiles, which helps keep tile edges flush with one another. A suction lifter makes it easier to handle heavy tiles, giving you a handle to grab to help with placement.

A suction lifter makes it easy to position large, heavy tiles or to lift tiles that need to be adjusted.

6 Combing thinset in one direction for each new section provides good adhesion for the next tiles.

TILING A ROOM (CONTINUED)

of the set tiles as a guide; of course, spacers are added to keep the grout lines between the tiles even ❺. If there's more than $1/16$ in. of size variation between tiles, we'll snap additional chalklines to keep the rows straight and true. We place a tile (with spacers) on each end of the last-set row ❻ and snap a line at their edges. This process is repeated for each row until all the full-size tiles are set ❼.

⚠ WARNING

Mixing thinset is a dusty, messy job that's best done outdoors. Always wear a dust mask and work clothes, as some thinset is bound to splatter—especially if you mix with an electric drill-powered paddle wheel.

5 Continue to set full tiles across the floor, using both the edges of the previously set tiles and the chalk layout lines as guides.

6 Additional chalklines serve as a guide to keep subsequent rows of tile straight.

7 We set only full tiles across the floor; the cut tiles will be set the next day.

TILING A STEP

In this example, the step between the entry and the living room is to be tiled, both along its edge and on the face of the step. Stair edges receive more abuse than the rest of the floor; this high-traffic area must be set with extra care.

To set the bullnose trim on the edge of the step, start by finding the center of the step to determine where the middle tile will be set. These trim tiles should overhang the edge enough to cover the tops of the vertically set tile on the riser. Then work outwards in both directions **❶**.

See "Methods of Planning Layout," p. 132.

Back-butter and set these tiles, using slightly more thin-set than usual **❷**. Be sure that there are no voids in your thinset; you want to get some squeeze-out to tell you there is enough setting material. Use a level or straightedge to make sure the bullnose tiles are flat and even with the field tiles **❸**. Scrape away any excess that has oozed under the front edge of the tile **❹**. Work your way across the step,

>> >> >>

The step is tiled **with a bullnose edge on top and a cut tile on the face of the riser.**

1 Use the center of the entry layout to determine the best layout pattern for the bullnose step trim.

2 Back-buttering each bullnose trim tile ensures that its bond with the concrete floor will be strong.

3 Use a small level to keep the bullnose tiles flat and even with the adjacent flooring.

4 Use a margin trowel to remove excess thinset from the overhanging edge of the trim tiles.

TILING A STEP (CONTINUED)

5 Continue down the edge of the step, setting the bullnose tiles level with one another and adding spacers as you go.

6 Add extra thinset to fill out voids behind the cut tiles that cover the face of the riser.

7 Use a torpedo level to make sure that the riser tiles are plumb and even with the edge of the bullnose tiles.

8 Place spacers and/or wedges under the riser tiles to adjust the grout joint at the top and form a caulk joint at the bottom.

setting the bullnose and cleaning any extra material from the front **5**. Allow these tiles to dry overnight. Cut the face tiles for the stair riser narrow enough to allow a grout joint at the top and the bottom of the tile. Set the tiles by both back-buttering them and adding additional thinset to the riser to make sure they are solidly set **6**. Use a torpedo level to make sure each tile is plumb and even with the bullnose tile set above it **7**. Add spacers and/or wedges as necessary to adjust the height of the face tiles **8**. When you later grout the step and riser, make sure to pack the grout fully into the joints.

SETTING CUT TILES

Because it's difficult to lean over freshly set field tiles without shifting them, we recommend scraping off thinset around those tiles, letting them dry, and saving the cuts for the next day. After waiting a full 24 hours, mark and cut the tiles.

> See "Marking Straight Cuts," "Marking Diagonal Cuts," and "Marking Complex Cuts," pp. 50-52.

> See "Through Cuts on the Wet Saw," "Cutting Curves," and "L-Shaped Cuts," pp. 56-59.

Before setting these tiles, place some rosin paper or other protective material over the floor tiles, to protect them against thinset drips. Scrape any dried thinset off the floor around the set tiles using your margin trowel ❶. Now dry-fit your cut tile and trim it as necessary with a pair of nippers or a water saw. Also be sure to use a rubbing stone on any cut tile edges that will show. Use a margin or notched trowel to apply thinset to the back of each tile and then set it in place ❷, ❸. If the tile is too low or too high, add or remove thinset until it fits into place, even with the adjacent tiles.

At doorways, it is easier to cut the bottom of the door casing to make room for the new tile rather than to trim the tile to go around the casing. First, make a shim that equals the thickness of the set floor tile and thinset by laying a scrap of tile atop a piece of thin wood or cardboard. Set the shim on the floor next to the casing, and mark a pencil line. Now use a small handsaw (an undercut or jambsaw works best) to cut the casing at the line ❹.

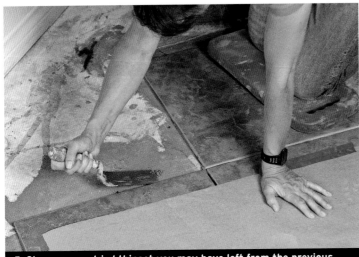

1 Clean up any dried thinset you may have left from the previous day before you attempt to fit the cut tiles.

2 Comb an even layer of thinset onto the back of the cut tiles with a notched trowel.

3 Carefully lay the back-buttered cut tile in place, aligning and leveling it relative to the adjacent tiles.

4 To set tile around doorways, first cut off the door casing, using a scrap tile, wood, or cardboard shim to support the saw.

SETTING TERRA-COTTA PAVERS

1 Before setting tiles, lay down a grid line so that you can fit nine tiles within each grid.

2 Wipe down your substrate with a damp sponge before spreading thinset.

3 Scoop a large amount of thinset onto the floor with a trowel.

4 Comb the thinset in one direction, using a ¹/₂-in. by ¹/₂-in. square or half-moon notched trowel.

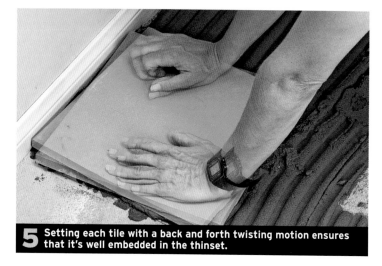

5 Setting each tile with a back and forth twisting motion ensures that it's well embedded in the thinset.

A grid of chalklines snapped across the floor makes laying irregular tiles, such as terra-cotta Saltillos, much easier. The lines allow you to cover the floor by laying tile in one nine-tile grid at a time. The grid creates a regular, orderly looking floor, despite the irregularities of the individual tiles within each grid **1**.

Clean the concrete (or substrate) with a damp sponge **2**. Scoop a big pile of thinset onto the floor **3**. Use a ¹/₂-in. by ¹/₂-in. square or half-moon notched trowel to spread and comb the thinset over the area you're working on, making sure not to completely obscure your layout lines **4**. Place the tile onto the floor, pressing it down and twisting it back and forth slightly to embed it thoroughly in the thinset **5**. Make sure the edge of the

6 Pavers are often not flat and thus require more thinset under them for a proper bond.

7 Use a trowel or margin trowel to lift tiles that aren't well seated in the thinset.

tile lines up with the chalkline, but leaves enough room for the grout joint.

You'll use more thinset to set pavers than with most other tiles. Because they're rarely flat, it takes more material to fill the hollow spaces under their concave or convex surfaces **6**. If a tile doesn't feel fully seated when it's set, use a margin trowel to lift it **7**, then check to see if the underside is fully coated **8**. If you have sparse coverage, add more thinset to fill any low areas or

>> >> >>

8 Uncoated areas on this tile show that it wasn't properly bonded to the floor.

SETTING TERRA-COTTA PAVERS (CONTINUED)

9 Add more thinset to the underside of the tile, comb it, then reset it.

10 Continue to set tiles within the grid, one row at a time.

11 Even up the space between tiles while the thinset is still wet.

12 Use a damp sponge to immediately wipe away thinset drips from the face of the tile.

13 Continue spreading thinset and setting tiles grid by grid, aligning them with the tiles in the adjacent row.

voids and reset the tile **9**. Continue setting the tiles in the row of your grid **10**. After you have filled each row, adjust the grout lines between the tiles **11**. The grout joints won't line up perfectly straight to one another, but after they are grouted, they will yield a consistent yet handmade look over the entire floor. Continue setting and adjusting tiles row by row, until the grid is full. Always wipe down the faces of the tiles before moving onto the next grid **12**. Even if you preseal the tiles, it is imperative to clean the faces of each tile, because dried thinset stains can be impossible to remove. Spread thinset in the next grid and repeat the process **13**. If your layout requires cut tiles, it's best to set these last, after the tiles set in the grids have dried.

➡ See "Setting Cut Tiles," p. 157.

SETTING POLISHED STONE

Unlike ceramic tiles, polished stone tiles require that each and every tile be set even and level with the tiles around it to achieve a flat, smooth floor. The relatively wide joints between ceramic tiles allow you to ramp the grout, to smooth out transitions between slightly uneven tiles; however, stone tiles are typically set with very narrow grout joints that don't allow ramping. Thus, it's very important for a floor or substrate under stone tiles to be absolutely flat and even.

➤ See "Applying Self-Leveling Compound," pp. 110–112.

In preparation for setting, tiles should be selected and, if desired, laid out and numbered for vein or color patterns ❶.

➤ See "Stone Tile Layout," p. 146.

All types of stone tiles need sealing before they're set.

➤ See "Sealing Natural Stone," p. 241.

When you're ready to lay the tiles, use a 1/2-in. by 1/2-in. half-moon trowel to spread a heavy layer of thinset over the floor. This thick layer will allow you to adjust each tile up or down relative to its neighbors ❷. Use medium-bed thinset so that it will not sag from the weight of the heavy tile ❸. After combing the thinset, set the first tile and then use a 6-in.

>> >> >>

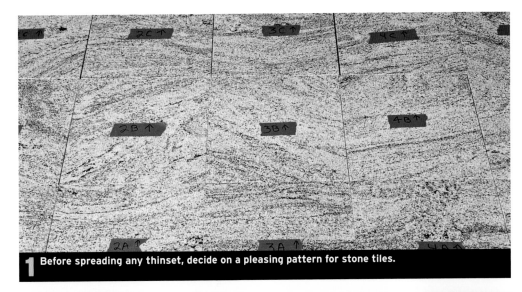

1 Before spreading any thinset, decide on a pleasing pattern for stone tiles.

2 Comb thinset with a large-notched trowel to allow adjustments for height variation.

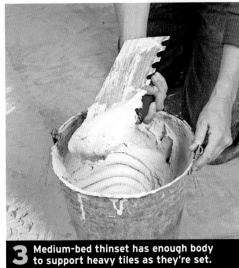

3 Medium-bed thinset has enough body to support heavy tiles as they're set.

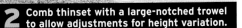
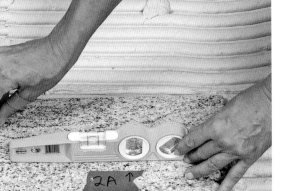

4 A small level helps adjust stone tiles so that they're level with one another.

SETTING POLISHED STONE (CONTINUED)

5 X-shape ¹⁄₁₆-in. spacers keep stone tiles properly aligned for even grout joints.

6 Tapping the tile with a mallet embeds it into the thinset.

7 If you find a high spot, adjust the tile with a mallet or your fingertips.

8 Back-butter cut stone tiles before setting them in place.

torpedo level to check that it's level, front to back and side to side **4**. Now set a tile next to it, using a ¹⁄₁₆-in. spacer set upright between the tiles **5**. Tap in the tile, using a mallet and level to set its surface flush with the adjacent tiles **6**. Rub your hands along the joint between the tiles as you set each new tile to feel that the surfaces are even **7**. After all the whole field tiles have been set and cured, you're ready to measure and set the cut tiles around the edges of the floor. Cover the previously set tiles with rosin paper to protect them as you work. Even though the tiles have been sealed, dried thinset is a bear to remove and can leave a mark on the surface of any highly polished stone. Mark and cut the tiles, then back-butter each one **8** and ease it into place, using a level and fingertips to check it for perfect placement.

AVOIDING STONE TILE PROBLEMS

A Never mark on the underside of light-colored marble tiles because marks may bleed through, as with this onyx tile.

B Brushing epoxy on the back of black, green, and red marble tiles prevents them from warping when set.

A floor set with 12-in.-sq. marble or granite tiles can lend elegance to any room. However, setting a smooth, flat floor of polished stone requires more time and effort than setting a ceramic tile floor. Since stone is a natural material it also requires more care than ceramic and terra-cotta tiles.

Never mark the back of any light-colored or translucent tile with an ink marker. The moisture from thinset when the tile is set can cause the ink to bleed through and show a reverse image on the surface of the tile **A**.

You must protect black, red, and green marble tiles from moisture, which can (believe it or not) cause them to curl or warp when they're laid with thinset. Coating the back of each tile with clear epoxy prevents moisture penetration still allowing the thinset to bond. Use a brush to completely cover the back of the tile, then set it aside to let the epoxy cure **B**.

Although we've seen marble floors with tiles that were butt set (set flush to each other), we don't recommend it. Butt-set tiles have only narrow V-shaped joints between them that are so shallow the grout eventually crumbles out of them. Grout manufacturers recommend leaving at least a $\frac{1}{16}$-in.-wide joint so the grout will have enough body and depth to achieve a good cure **C**.

C A $\frac{1}{16}$-in.-wide grout joint is the smallest that's advisable when setting a stone tile floor.

LARGE-FORMAT TILES

In years past, the trend was toward smaller and smaller tiles including mosaics. Recently, the move has been in the other direction—toward supersizing the size of tiles, with no real limit in sight. In general, any tile over 15 in. x 15 in. is considered a large-format tile (LF); however, wood-look plank tiles that are narrower on one side and over 15 in. on the other are also considered to be large-format tiles (see p. 23). For our local tile business, installing 12-in. x 24-in. tiles has become a large part of our work. And now, there are even tiles that are over 4 ft. x 8 ft. as well as ceramic and porcelain tile panels that are even larger. With all of these larger tiles, there is less grout to clean, resulting in a cleaner, more expansive look.

Installing large-format tiles

Working with LF tiles presents some challenges that smaller tiles do not. Because tile does not bend, it's imperative that your substrate be as flat as possible. We've all experienced floors where this issue was not addressed and tripped lightly over "lippage." The American National Standards Institute (ANSI) specification for installing large-format ceramic tile recommends that the substrate have no more than $1/8$ in. in 10-ft. variance, with no more than $1/16$-in. variation in 24 in. In the leveling section of the book (pp. 110–112), we explain in detail how to create a flat and level floor. With any job that requires leveling, we strongly suggest hiring a licensed professional for areas over 100 sq. ft.

Even with a properly flattened substrate, warped LF tiles can lead to lippage, which is where leveling clips come in (see p. 165). When you use the clips, adjacent tiles are lifted or lowered to make an even plane. You'll need to use more thinset than usual ($1/16$ in. to $1/8$ in. more) to allow room for the clips, tile, and thinset to work together.

Spread large-format thinset with a bigger notched trowel than usual to allow for the leveling clips under the tile.

Today's tiles may be larger **than the people who lift them.**

TRADE SECRET
Large-format (LF) tiles are any tiles over 15 in. on any side. If you consider working with this size, look for tiles that are "rectified" (see p. 39). They give a "clean and lean" look with a more uniform tile size and sharp, narrow grout joints.

TRADE SECRET
Before you install 12-in. x 24-in. wood plank, or any LF tile in a staggered or brick pattern, check with the manufacturer about the amount of overlap. Most manufacturers recommend a 33% overlap rather than 50% overlap. If you choose to install with a 50% overlap, just be aware that you may experience some shadowing or lippage from tile to tile.

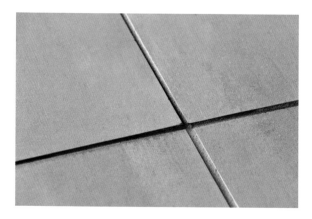

Tiles that are not even with each other **create a condition known as "lippage."**

BACK-BUTTERING LARGE-FORMAT TILES

Back-buttering is applying thinset to the underside of a tile to ensure complete coverage between the thinset on the substrate and the tile.

With larger tiles, you must always back-butter the underside of each tile. Tiles need to be supported by enough thinset, especially larger tiles, which are prone to warpage. Larger tiles also become unwieldy to beat and embed properly into a bed of thinset unless they are first back-buttered. In addition, back-buttering provides extra insurance against cracks in your tile.

Insert the leveling stem **at the intersection of two tiles and set the next two tiles.**

Back-butter the tile and set it in the thinset bed. For the twist-type clips, insert the leveler at the corner. Back-butter and lay your next tile and, when the clip is covered (three tiles for T-shape levelers and four tiles for X-shape levelers), twist on the cap and tighten securely. For the wedge-type clip, place the clips at the corners and insert the wedge into the clip after you've laid clips for the adjacent tiles (see the photos on p. 167).

Use a mallet to beat the tiles in after you've tightened the clips. Periodically check that the tiles have not slipped out of alignment. Also use your mallet to tap the edges if you need to adjust the tile into alignment or to keep it within the chalk line. Continue tiling, adding clips and/or spacers as you go.

The following day, or at least 24 hours later (to allow the thinset to cure), kick out the clips or use a mallet. All clips are designed to break off cleanly when broken in the direction of the grout joint. If a clip does not break off cleanly (a rare occurrence), use your utility knife and a sharp new blade to carefully carve the clip below the surface of the tile. You may also pull gently, wriggling carefully with long-nose or other pliers to extricate it from the joint.

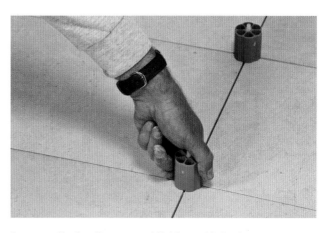

Screw on the leveling cap **and tighten until the faces are even.**

Use a mallet or your foot **to kick out the clips.**

PLANK FLOORING

In many homes, wood-look tiles have replaced wood flooring. That's because they are much more durable, won't scratch, and require less maintenance than wood, especially over time. Because of their growing popularity, the choices are almost infinite in color, texture, patterns, and size.

The customary size range is 4 in. to 9 in. in width and from 2 ft. to 5 ft. in length. Use a narrower grout line because less grout means less to maintain and it gives a cleaner look. As with all large-format tiles, you'll need to be mindful of the manufacturer's 33% overlap cautions to avoid lippage and have a trouble-free installation.

Installing plank flooring

Level the floor so that the planks will lay as flat as possible (see pp. 110–112). For any installation, you should also install an antifracture or uncoupling membrane to ensure that your tiles will not crack (see pp. 72–74).

After you've planned your layout according to the width of the tile (from front to back of the room), you're ready to start. The length of the room will not matter as the lengths of the tile ends will be randomized.

Snap a chalkline lengthwise but no farther than 2 ft. from your starting edge or as far as you can comfortably reach. Spread thinset beyond the length of the tile and up to the chalkline. Back-butter the first tile and place it onto the bed of thinset ❶. Place leveling clips at the corners and edges of the tile before you lay your next tile. Cut, back-butter, and set a tile for the second row that will allow for no more than one-third overlap of the previous tile ❷. Save the rest of that cut tile and use it for the other side or another row. Cut, back-butter, and place your third row tile, and if you can use a previously cut tile, do so, being mindful of the one-third overlap of each tile ❸. Be sure to tighten the leveling clips. Seat all tiles by tapping lightly with your mallet ❹.

1 Comb the thinset on the underlayment in one direction. Back-butter each tile before setting it in the thinset.

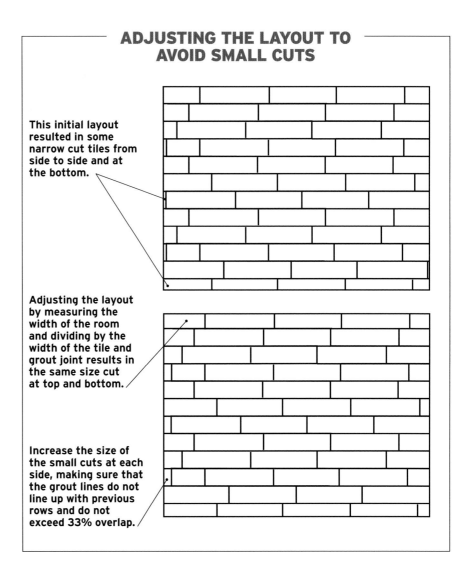

ADJUSTING THE LAYOUT TO AVOID SMALL CUTS

This initial layout resulted in some narrow cut tiles from side to side and at the bottom.

Adjusting the layout by measuring the width of the room and dividing by the width of the tile and grout joint results in the same size cut at top and bottom.

Increase the size of the small cuts at each side, making sure that the grout lines do not line up with previous rows and do not exceed 33% overlap.

2 Lay the first tile, add leveling spacers, and then place the next tile.

3 Cut your third row tile, being careful not to exceed 33% overlap. Add spacers and set the tile.

4 Use a mallet to beat the tile in place.

5 If you're finished for the day, place levelers at the last row, and other spacers underneath scrap tile as if it was set.

6 Push the wedges in tight. This process will help you avoid dips in the floor when you return to lay the rest of the tile.

7 The next day, kick out the spacers in the direction of the grout joint. Or knock them out with a mallet.

Before moving on to the next section, place a couple of wedges or spacers against the wall to prevent the tiles from sliding out of adjustment. Tap across the front edge of the tiles to ensure that the tiles are tight up against the spacers and make sure you can see your chalkline. Spread the next section and continue to place tiles until you reach the end of this section. Snap another chalkline three to four lines down based on your reachable depth and continue until you reach the end of that row. At each new section, be sure that you are measuring your cuts to overlap no more than one-third of the tile in the previous row.

At the day's end, if it's a small room, you won't be able to finish the area that you are tiling because it becomes very awkward to reach and set these large tiles. You'll need to finish laying the floor the next day when you can kneel on the previously set tiles. Either way, small or large area, finish the areas you have tiled by inserting leveling clips, tile scraps, and spacers (to mimic the height of the thinset) **5**, **6**. In this way, you'll keep the tile height of your last section ready for the tiles you'll set the following day. Failure to do this may allow the edge of this last row of tiles to dip slightly and cause lippage between those two rows. The next day, begin by removing the leveling clips **7** and then clean this area thoroughly before setting the next section.

HEATED FLOORS

Heated floors used to be considered a luxury, but these days home-owners everywhere (yes, even in sunny California and other hot spots) are tempted by the idea of toasty toes year-round. Heated floors are energy efficient and easy to install, and the temperature can be set to match your schedule with a programmable thermostat. There are a variety of companies producing heating systems, but the premade pad is the simplest for DIYers to install. There are other options, such as systems or kits in which you string your own wires using proprietary fasteners, but these require experienced installers as the wires cannot be cut and have to fit the space perfectly.

Installing a heated floor pad

Some companies offer a number of standard-size pads that are readily available, or you may want to order a custom-size or -shaped pad for your particular space. Before you begin any actual work, you first need to measure your floor area accurately, create a simple drawing of the room, and send it to the manufacturer. For the floor shown here, we used a heated pad from Nuheat®.

From your drawing, the manufacturer will create and send back a plan of your room to verify dimensions, placement of cabinets, toilet, and so on. Once approved, they will ship your custom pad direct to you.

Heated floor pads (also known as radiant floor heating mats) **are laid under your tile and act like an electric blanket to warm up the floor tiles. Shown here are the tools you'll need to install one, including (from left to right) an electrician's fish tape, wood and carbide chisels, a glue gun, an alarm mechanism, and an ohm multimeter. The Nuheat mat with wires is shown at rear.**

ROOM LAYOUT FOR HEATED FLOOR PAD

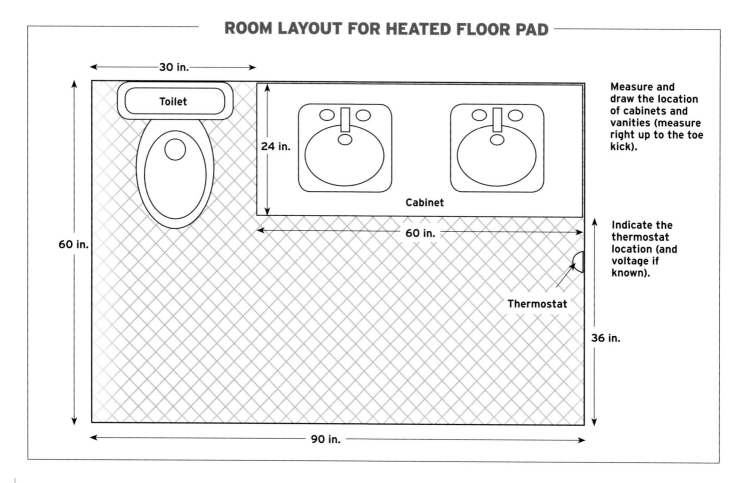

If you have enough space, **leave the pad un-furled and/or dampen with a wet sponge if necessary to get it to lie flat before installation.**

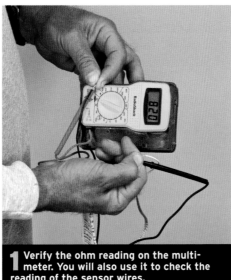

1 Verify the ohm reading on the multi-meter. You will also use it to check the reading of the sensor wires.

2 Attach the lead wires of the heating pad to the end of an electrical fish tape.

While you're waiting for the pad to arrive, alert your electrician to run the wiring per the manufacturer's directions. Be sure to have two conduit drops: one for the sensor, one for the power leads. Once the pad arrives, roll it out in place to verify that it fits properly.

The first step is to verify the ohm reading with a multimeter ❶. The manufacturer will supply a tag that has the desired range for your ohm reading. (Each mat reading is different and varies according to the square footage.) Now you can pull the lead wires of the pad into the junction box ❷, ❸. Attach the alert mechanism, which will alert you if you inadvertently damage the pad or cut any wires while installing the mat or tiles ❹. Leave the mechanism on until after the floor is grouted. Roll out the heating pad in the space ❺.

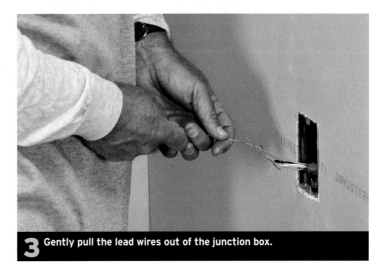

3 Gently pull the lead wires out of the junction box.

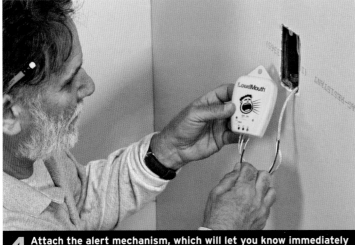

4 Attach the alert mechanism, which will let you know immediately if a wire has been cut.

5 Roll out the heating pad for a test fit.

HEATED FLOORS (CONTINUED)

6 Move the pad aside and comb the thinset in one direction.

7 Place the pad in place and use a wood or rubber float to embed it in the thinset.

8 Spread the rest of the area with thinset, and roll out the pad onto the new area.

9 Carefully chisel out a small depression to allow the temperature sensor to sit below the level of the heating wires.

10 Hot-glue the sensor in place and use small pieces of tape to hold the wires in place.

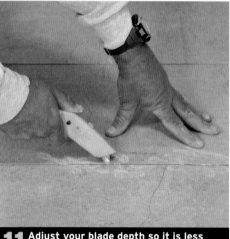

11 Adjust your blade depth so it is less than the thickness of the wire.

Move the pad out of the way and comb thinset onto the substrate **6**. Place the pad back in place and use a rubber or wood float to embed the pad in the thinset **7**. Continue until the entire pad is adhered to the substrate **8**.

Use a chisel to chip out a shallow channel in the backerboard or concrete substrate for the temperature sensor **9**. Hot-glue the sensor in place and tape the wires down to the pad as you run them back to the second conduit drop **10**.

Run the wires back up to the junction box and check the continuity of the sensor with the multimeter. Install the tile with care, making sure the alert mechanism is always on. After the tile is installed, you'll want to clean the grout joints but use great caution that you do not cut a wire. The best way to do this is to retract the utility knife blade to its shallowest depth **11**, or use a small cleaning brush **12**. Grout the tile as usual, allow cure time, and enjoy your heated floor.

12 Alternatively, you can use a hard bristle brush to clean the joints.

SETTING TILE BASE AND TRIM

A baseboard installed around the perimeter of a floor protects the walls from dents and scuffs due to brooms, vacuum cleaners, and other everyday wear ❶. Tile base goes on after the floor is completely set but before it is grouted. If the base tiles are the same size as the field tiles, align the grout joints. Otherwise, find the center point of each wall and lay out the base tiles symmetrically, to yield the biggest cut pieces on either end. Back-butter each base piece and press it onto the wall surface ❷, ❸. Use a spacer or wedge to raise the base off the floor, to leave room for a caulk joint. Remember to fill this joint with caulk, not grout, as walls and floors can flex and move at different rates, causing grout to crack.

If you're installing a wood base, you'll want to nail it in place after the floor and grout are completely set. It's best to stain or paint the wood before you set it in place to avoid drips or stains on your new tile floor. The nail holes will be easy to touch up.

TRADE SECRET
If your chosen tile does not come with a surface bullnose that can be used as base trim, you can always cut a field tile to the desired height and set it with the cut edge down.

1 Tile base adds a nice finish to a tile floor and protects the bottom edge of the wall.

2 Back-butter each base tile with modified thinset.

3 Press the tile base onto the wall, using spacers to keep the tops even to one another and to allow a caulk joint below.

INSTALLING EDGING

You'll need to measure the thickness of your tile to help you select the appropriate-size edge trim. Another option is to take your tile to the store with you so that you can hold the trim piece in place to find the right size. Ideally, you want the tile and the trim piece to be as close as possible in size. Some companies offer a gauge tool that measures the thickness of the tile and is marked with the size of the matching trim you need.

Your tile store may have **a gauge to measure the thickness of your tile to match it with the appropriate-size edge trim.**

→ See "Transition and Edge Trim," pp. 92–93.

Measure and cut your edge trim piece to the length you need ❶. A new hacksaw blade will help to prevent skittering, but, in any case, take your time because the metal surface cannot be repaired. You can also use a tile saw to cut some softer metals or plastic edging. A tile rubbing stone can be used to smooth burrs ❷.

Apply thinset and set the tile base. Slide the edge trim piece behind the tile while the thinset is workable ❸. Use wedges or spacers to keep the grout line consistent between the tile and the trim. Wedges are also handy to adjust the trim against an irregular adjacent surface and to match the face of the tile ❹.

After the thinset has cured, use a sponge or small scrub brush to clean the joints. Don't use a razor knife as one slip could mar your beautiful trim and replacing it at this stage is very difficult. Grout as usual.

1 Measure, and then use a hacksaw to cut the trim to length.

2 Use a rubbing stone to remove and smooth any burrs.

3 Insert the trim piece behind the tile base while the thinset is still workable.

Some lines of trim **have inside or outside corners. Install these first and measure accordingly.**

4 Wedges can be a great tool to help you adjust the trim.

TRIMMING FLOOR TRANSITIONS

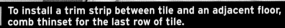

1 To install a trim strip between tile and an adjacent floor, comb thinset for the last row of tile.

2 Press the perforated edge of the trim firmly into the thinset.

3 Set tiles along the edge of the trim strip, leaving room for a caulk joint.

Often, a new tile floor butts up against an existing floor at a doorway or hall. If the tile is higher than the adjacent floor, you can sometimes use surface bullnose or quarter-round trim to finish off the edge. A more versatile solution is to install a metal trim strip. Schluter brand trim comes in different profiles and colors to suit transitions between tile and wood, carpet, and other kinds of flooring. Installing this trim is much like setting tile. Start by laying down a strip of masking tape to protect the finished floor adjacent to the tile **1**. Spread the thinset onto your substrate, in preparation for setting the last row of tile. Cut the trim strip to length and press its perforated edge firmly into the thinset **2**. Align the strip with the edge of the finished flooring. Mark and cut the tiles to fit against the trim strip, leaving room for a caulk joint. Place these tiles into the thinset as you would normally set any floor tile **3**. Before the thinset firms up, adjust the profile so that the grout joint is parallel and consistent with the floor tile. Let this dry for 24 hours and then grout the tile floor, leaving the joint between the metal trim strip and the tile open. Caulking this joint allows for movement between the two different floor materials.

BASIC COUNTERTOP WITH BULLNOSE EDGE

The bullnose tile **overhangs the tile below.**

1 Mark where the back side of the edge titles will fall.

B egin by marking the setback for the first row of tiles **❶**. In this case, the bullnose edge tile overhangs the tile beneath.

➡ **See "Laying Out Edges," p. 134.**

Hold a level or straightedge in place against the layout line and comb the thinset for the bullnose edge onto the front edge of the countertop **❷**. Place the tiles onto the thinset, then twist in place **❸**. If the tile is mesh mounted, you can check the spacing of the bullnose tiles against a row of field tiles **❹**. If not, use the single field tiles and spacers, if appropriate, to make certain the bullnose will line up with the field tile. Occasionally, the bullnose and field tile appear to be the same width, but a closer measurement will show that one is slightly larger. On a long counter, the bullnose can lose its alignment with the field tile. To make up for this, either expand or shrink the grout joints between the bullnose to match the field tile. Once grouted, this slight difference will not show. You may also notice that trim and field tiles have a range of shade variations between them **❺**. If you find noticeable color differences between the tiles, mix up the arrangement of trim tiles so they blend in **❻**.

After the edge row of bullnose tiles is set, spread and comb thinset over the rest of the countertop **❼**. If the area is larger than what you can cover in 10 minutes to 15 minutes, spread just part of the counter. Set the field tiles onto the thinset, lining them up with the bullnose tiles **❽**. Set the remaining tile, marking and making any cuts you need to fit tile where the counter meets the wall **❾**.

》》》

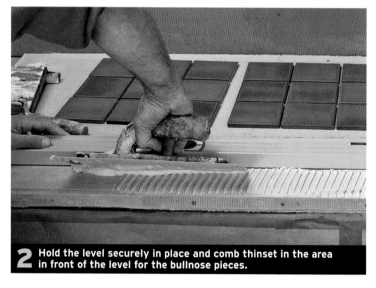

2 Hold the level securely in place and comb thinset in the area in front of the level for the bullnose pieces.

3 Use a level to help keep the bullnose tiles in a straight line as you press them in place.

4 Check the spacing on the bullnose tiles against a row of field tiles. Adjust as necessary.

5 The color of the trim tiles may vary widely from that of the field tiles.

6 Mixing up the tiles will help blend color variations that may otherwise stand out.

7 You can spread an entire small countertop with thinset at one time.

8 Set the field tiles into the thinset, lining them up with the first row of bullnose tiles.

9 Press the remaining tiles into place.

BASIC COUNTERTOP WITH BULLNOSE EDGE (CONTINUED)

Take a hammer and tap on a beating block to embed all the field and bullnose tiles in the thinset, seating them even to one another **10**. Use your fingertips to adjust any tiles that may have become misaligned **11**. Now set a level or straightedge against the front edge bullnose tiles **12** and straighten any tiles that have come out of line **13**. Set the rest of the countertop tile and let the installation dry for 24 hours before installing the edge trim.

10 To ensure that the tiles are all even with one another, tap them with a beating block.

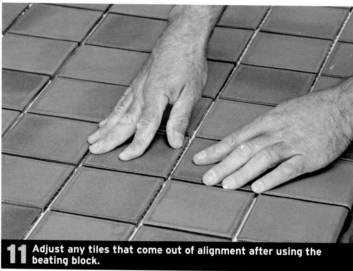

11 Adjust any tiles that come out of alignment after using the beating block.

12 Use a level to straighten the front row of bullnose tiles.

13 Straighten out any misaligned tiles.

EDGE TRIM UNDER OVERHANGING BULLNOSE

1 Apply a generous amount of thinset with a margin trowel onto the cut trim tiles.

2 Insert wedges or spacers to maintain an even grout joint with the bullnose tile.

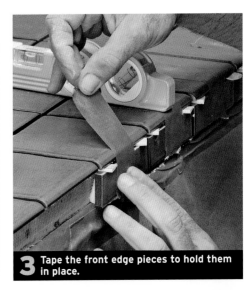

3 Tape the front edge pieces to hold them in place.

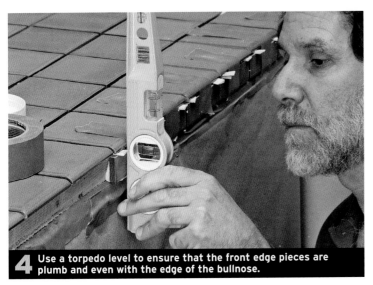

4 Use a torpedo level to ensure that the front edge pieces are plumb and even with the edge of the bullnose.

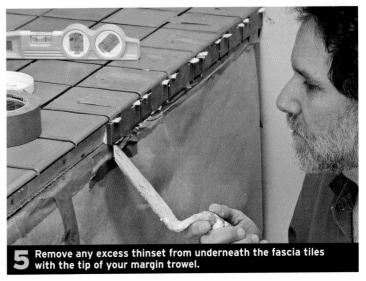

5 Remove any excess thinset from underneath the fascia tiles with the tip of your margin trowel.

Cut field tiles to fit under the surface bullnose. You'll need to be sure that the size of the tile you cut will clear any drawers, built-in bread boards, door fronts, and the dishwasher. Also, before you mark the tiles, remember to allow for a grout joint or a spacer.

Mix up a small batch of slightly stiff thinset. This consistency will make it easier for you to set the face pieces and for them to hold fast in place. Back-butter the cut face pieces **1** and press into place under the bullnose, using spacers or wedges as necessary **2**. You must have enough thinset to get some goosh out on the sides but not so much to cause them to sit beyond the bullnose edge. Use tape to hold the face tiles in place and prevent them from sliding **3**. Use a torpedo level to keep the faces plumb and even with the bull-nose **4**. Carefully remove any excess thinset from underneath the face tiles with your margin trowel **5**.

TRADE SECRET
If the face pieces are too heavy for the tape to hold them, use some finish nails underneath their bottom edge. Nail these into the face frame of the cabinet and use wedges as necessary to adjust them. You can fill the nail holes later, after you grout.

L- OR U-SHAPED COUNTERTOP

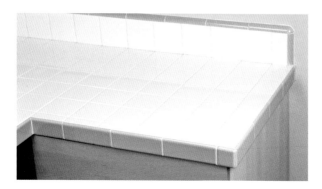

In this example, the edge trim **covers the front edge of the perimeter tiles.**

Setting tile on an L- or U-shaped peninsula countertop involves setting rows of tile straight and square to the rows running across the main countertop. Set the field tile along the edge of the main countertop first. In this example, the first row of tiles will sit behind the edge trim. Make sure that the first row is set flush with the front edge of the substrate. Begin by holding a level or straightedge in place against the layout line and comb the thinset for the edge onto the front edge of the countertop.

➜ See photo 2 on p. 178.

Now lay the first full-size row of field tiles on the peninsula counter, using a framing square to keep it perpendicular to the tile on the main countertop **❶**. Continue with the remaining uncut field tiles, tapping them in place with the bottom of your fist or a rubber mallet **❷**.

Then check the edges of the two counters, to see if they are square with one another **❸**. If they are square, proceed to laying the remainder of the tile.

1 Use a framing square to set the field tiles perpendicular to the tile on the main counter.

2 Lay the remainder of the L-shaped countertop, tapping the tiles in place.

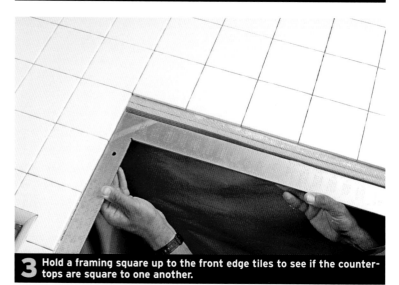

3 Hold a framing square up to the front edge tiles to see if the countertops are square to one another.

DEALING WITH AN OUT-OF-SQUARE COUNTERTOP

You can leave the edge tiles **straight and compensate by filling the space of the overhang with thinset when setting trim.**

1 Check for square. In an out-of-square cabinet, straight-cut tiles will overhang the edge at one end.

2 To determine the taper, mark the tile on one end to line up with the counter edge.

3 Then mark the opposite end.

If your L- or U-shaped countertop is not square and your edge tiles overhang, there are two ways you can proceed: The first is to cut all of the first-row tiles to the same width so that part of the row overhangs the edge slightly. You end up with a row of same-width tiles that effectively hides the cabinet's out-of-square edge. When you set trim on this edge, you simply add extra thinset to the backs of the tiles to space them far enough out from the cabinet face to line up with the cut field tiles.

The second method is to cut the tiles that run along the front edge of the peninsula counter at a taper, so that they'll follow the out-of-square front edge **1**. This allows you to set the rest of the field tiles square to the front row. To cut the tapered tiles so that they fit accurately, start by cutting all the tiles you need for the edge slightly wider than the final size, and lay them in place dry. Now mark each of the tiles at the ends of the countertop even with the front edge of the cabinet **2**, **3**. >> >> >>

DEALING WITH AN OUT-OF-SQUARE COUNTERTOP (CONTINUED)

4 Tape the tiles to hold them steady and to provide a surface for your pencil line.

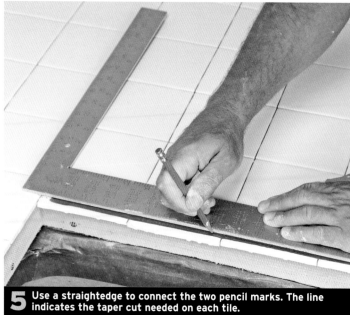

5 Use a straightedge to connect the two pencil marks. The line indicates the taper cut needed on each tile.

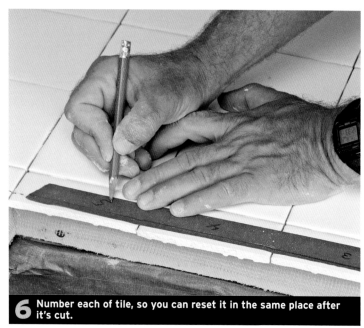

6 Number each of tile, so you can reset it in the same place after it's cut.

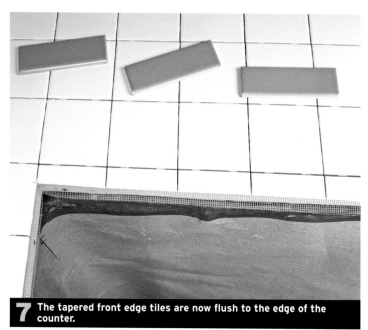

7 The tapered front edge tiles are now flush to the edge of the counter.

Lay a piece of blue tape across all of the top field tiles to give you an easy surface to mark. This will also keep the tiles in place while you mark them **4**. Take a straightedge and draw a line, connecting the two outside marks **5**. This will be your cut line for the tiles. Label the tiles in the order that you'll set them and cut them on the water saw or cutting board **6**. The finished tapered edge is now flush to the countertop **7**.

SETTING FLUSH-TO-TOP EDGE TRIM

To set the bullnose edge trim on the countertop's edge, back-butter each trim piece with thinset, press it in place, then secure it with tape so it doesn't shift as the thinset dries ❶. Check the face of each tile as you set it with a torpedo level, to make sure that it's plumb ❷.

Cut and set the two mitered bullnose edge tiles that meet at the inside corner of the counter. Cut these tiles by holding them on edge while cutting on a water saw ❸. Use a square-edged scrap 2x4 to keep the tile perpendicular to the blade. Set a mitered bullnose tile on one side of the corner first, then push the second corner piece in place, adjusting the fit as necessary until the trim appears even ❹.

Outside corners of a bullnose-trimmed counter are usually finished with bullnose outside down angles, instead of two mitered pieces. You can set these either of two ways: With the rounded bullnose corner on the long side of the counter ❺, or on the end

>> >> >>

1 Duct tape keeps the bullnose edge tiles from slipping as the thinset dries.

2 Check the front bullnose edge trim for plumb with a small level.

3 Use a piece of 2x4 to keep bullnose trim on edge while mitering the end.

4 Two mitered bullnose trim tiles form the inside corner of the countertop.

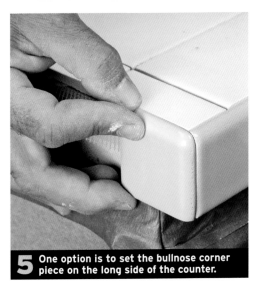

5 One option is to set the bullnose corner piece on the long side of the counter.

TRADE SECRET

If you're setting bullnose edge trim with a grout joint that's 1/8 in. or larger, use a spacer to create the joint between the bullnose and the field tiles on the countertop.

SETTING FLUSH-TO-TOP EDGE TRIM (CONTINUED)

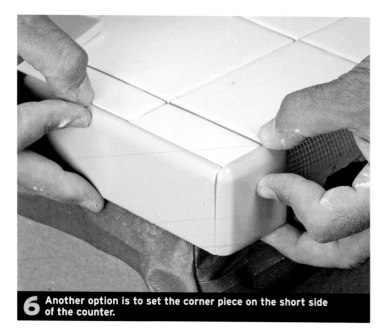

6 Another option is to set the corner piece on the short side of the counter.

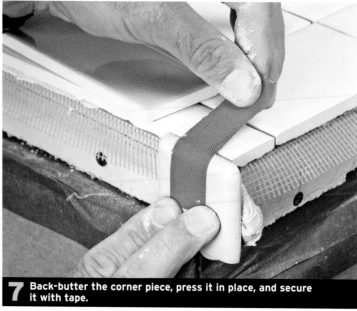

7 Back-butter the corner piece, press it in place, and secure it with tape.

8 Set the adjacent bullnose trim tile flush with the corner tile.

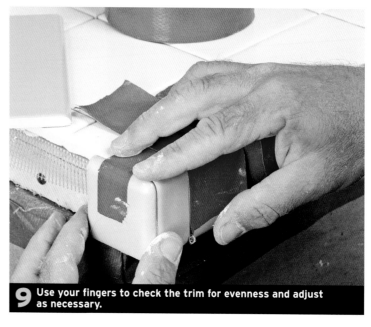

9 Use your fingers to check the trim for evenness and adjust as necessary.

of the counter **6**. Both are correct; it's up to your personal preference. Whichever orientation you choose, set the corner piece first **7**, then the regular bullnose trim next to it **8**. Feel the tops and sides of the tiles and adjust them until they're even **9**.

OVERMOUNT SINK COUNTERTOP

Start by marking and cutting the tiles that go around the perimeter of the sink cutout. Lay the tiles out along the front edge of the sink cutout, per the layout that yields the larger cut tiles along the sides of the sink.

 See "Laying Out a Sink Counter," p. 135.

In this example, the better layout starts with a grout joint in the middle, with a tile on either side of it ❶. Mark the width of the cut tiles that'll form a row on both sides of the sink, as well as the cut tiles that will be set at the front of the sink, using your layout lines. Also mark the L-shaped cuts for the tiles at the corners of the sink. By making the inside corner of the cut curved instead of square ❷, you'll prevent cracks that sometimes occur in these corner tiles. Cut all the tiles to size and make sure your layout will work ❸.

>> >> >>

TRADE SECRET
Regular gray thinset is fine for tile that will be grouted with dark grout. But it's best to use white thinset with tiles that will be grouted with a light-colored grout and when installing glass tiles.

1 Starting with a grout joint in the center, mark the width of the cut tiles that will run along either edge of the sink.

2 Mark the L-shaped tile that goes at the corner of the sink.

3 The tile around an overmount sink should be even and symmetrical.

INSTALLING A SINK

After you've grouted the counter and let it cure for 2 days to 3 days, you (or your plumber) can set your sink on top of the tile. Always set the sink with caulk to form a waterproof line around the sink that remains flexible. If you cannot get color-matched caulk, use clear instead.

Run a small bead of caulk around the perimeter of the sink opening on the counter ❶. Then lower the sink into the opening until it is seated ❷. Use a damp, clean sponge to wipe off any excess caulk and shape the caulk against the sink rim ❸.

1 Apply a bead of caulking on the tiles that surround the overmount sink's perimeter to provide a waterproof seal.

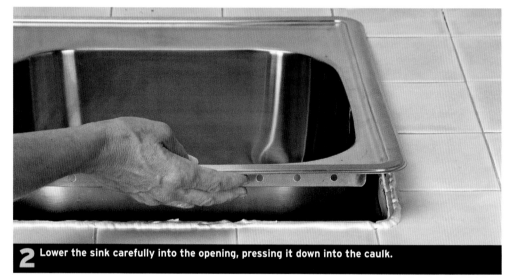

2 Lower the sink carefully into the opening, pressing it down into the caulk.

3 Use a damp sponge to wipe the excess caulk from around the sink.

TILING AN UNDERMOUNT SINK COUNTER

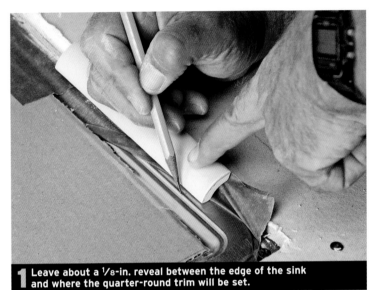

1 Leave about a 1/8-in. reveal between the edge of the sink and where the quarter-round trim will be set.

2 Hold a piece of quarter-round in place and mark its outside edge to indicate the outside edge of the sink trim.

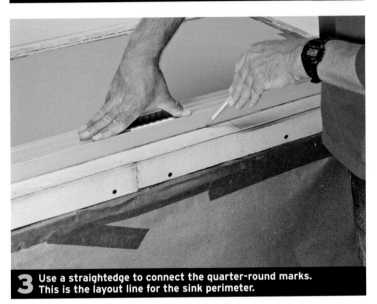

3 Use a straightedge to connect the quarter-round marks. This is the layout line for the sink perimeter.

4 After cutting the field tiles that frame the sink, use a rubbing stone on their cut edges to round them slightly.

Setting the countertop tiles when you have an undermount sink adds a few more steps to the work required for an over-mount sink. The main difference is that you will need additional trim tiles—bullnose or quarter-round—to finish around the sink.

You'll need to prepare the sink area in a particular manner. Please read the information on preparation for an undermount sink carefully.

➡️ **See "Undermount Sink with Quarter-Round Trim," p. 128.**

Before you cut and set your countertop tiles, you must determine how much room you need for the trim tiles to be set around the

sink. Hold the trim up to the sink, leaving about a 1/8-in. reveal (gap) between the trim and the inside sink edge, and make a pencil mark on the sink **1**. Also mark the outside edge of the trim onto the backerboard to indicate where the rows of field tile will meet the trim **2**. Do this on adjacent sides at all four corners of the sink. Now lay a level or straightedge on the backerboard marks and outline the sink on all sides **3**. This outline shows you where the field tiles that surround the sink will be set.

Cut the tiles that go around the sink, then use a rubbing stone on their edges to smooth them, as these edges will show **4**. Spread thinset around the sink and set the cut tiles, taking care not to

>> >> >>

TILING AN UNDERMOUNT SINK COUNTER (CONTINUED)

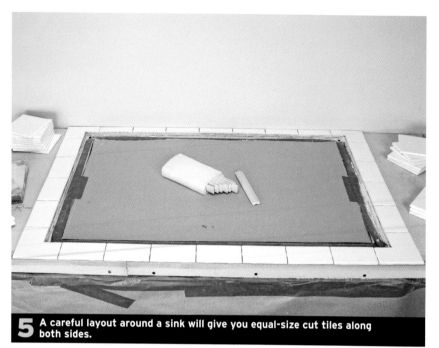

5 A careful layout around a sink will give you equal-size cut tiles along both sides.

6 Choose the layout for the sink trim tiles that gives you the biggest cut tiles at the corners of the sink.

obscure your pencil marks with thinset. Make sure the tiles are set square at the front and back, and that the front tiles are parallel to the sink and cabinet **5**.

To lay out the quarter-round sink trim, mark the centerline of the sink and start laying trim, beginning with either a full tile or a grout joint in the center **6**.

➡ See "Laying Out a Sink Counter," p. 135.

When you reach the corner, hold a trim tile in place and mark it for the cut **7**. Unless there are special corner trim pieces available, you'll need to miter the ends of two quarter-rounds for the corner. Cut the miters on a water saw, then use a stone on the cut edges. Back-butter with thinset and press the trim in place **8**. Repeat for all four sink edges until complete **9**. The completed sink installation, framed by tile is shown in photo **10**.

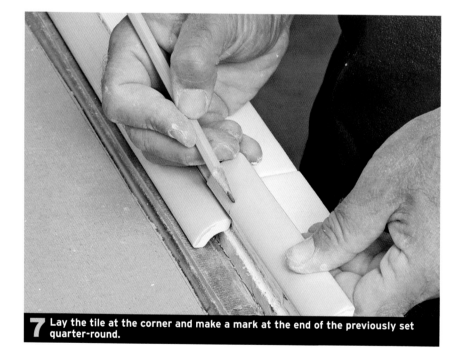

7 Lay the tile at the corner and make a mark at the end of the previously set quarter-round.

8 Use a margin trowel to fill the hollow on the underside of each quarter-round before setting it.

9 The mitered trim tiles should create a clean corner, with a consistent grout line where the miters meet.

10 The finished installation.

BEFORE YOU BEGIN

Before starting on your backsplash, you'll need the field tiles, trim and/or decorative tiles, plastic wedges, and spacers. You'll also need thinset, water, and perhaps a fortifying additive to blend it with. If you've made repairs or installed backerboard, be sure to tape all the seams ❶. When using tile smaller than 2 in. sq., it's especially important that the wall is flat. If necessary, fill hollow spots with quick-setting wall patch compound ❷.

➜ See "Backsplash Wall Repair and Prep," p. 120 and "Flattening the Wall," p. 121.

If your design calls for decorative tiles, make sure you decide on your layout before setting the tile ❸.

Before tiling a backsplash, it's important to cover sinks with a soft towel or blanket, then set a piece of backerboard or plywood on top, for protection. Protect the rest of the countertop with towels, tarps, or drop cloths ❹.

You can mix thinset either by hand or with a drill and paddle wheel. The hand method is good for mixing the small batches you'll likely need for simpler backsplash installations. Make sure to break up any lumps and thoroughly mix in any dry material that clings to the side or bottom of the bucket ❺.

➜ See "Mixing Thinset," p. 81.

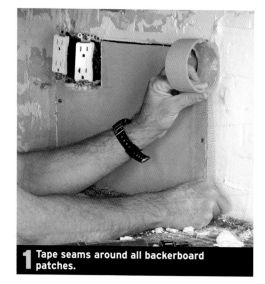

1 Tape seams around all backerboard patches.

2 Flatten the wall by filling hollows with quick-setting wall patch compound.

3 Decide on the layout for any decorative tile or trim.

4 Protect a sink with soft towels and cardboard.

5 Mix thinset until it has a smooth and even consistency.

BACKSPLASH WITH SURFACE BULLNOSE TRIM

1 Back-butter each bullnose trim piece with a margin trowel before pressing it to the wall.

2 Line each bullnose up with the grout line on the countertop below it.

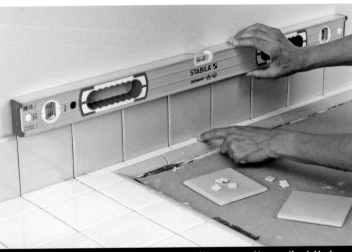

3 Level the tiles to keep them even with one another; adjust their height with wedges.

4 A single row of surface bullnose trim tiles makes a very nice short backsplash that's quick and easy to set.

A single row of surface bullnose trim tile can make a very nice short backsplash. For this installation, it's easier to back-butter each individual tile **1** than to trowel thinset on the wall. If the tiles are the same size as the field tiles used on the countertop, align the grout joints of the tiles where they meet **2**. Use wedges under the backsplash tiles **3** both to level them (the tops of the tiles should be straight and even) and to create a joint between the backsplash and the counter, which you'll caulk later. The finished backsplash has a clean simple look and provides the wall with protection against water spray from the sink **4**.

➔ See "Applying Caulk," p. 236.

BACKSPLASH WITH QUARTER-ROUND TRIM

1 Line up the grout joints of the backsplash tiles with the countertop tiles.

2 Mark the position of the quarter-round tile at the finished end of the backsplash.

3 Use the quarter-round position line to mark the field tile to be cut to size.

4 This beak–a quarter-round trim with a round end–is set along the top of the short backsplash to finish off the corner.

If the edges and ends of a tile backsplash will be finished with a quarter-round (or other radius trim), the first step is to cut and install backerboard on the wall.

➔ See "Backerboard on a Backsplash," p. 129.

Spread thinset on the backerboard and set the first row of field tiles, lining up their grout joints with the countertop tiles (if the tiles are the same size) **1**. Make sure this row is level and adjust the tiles with wedges or spacers as necessary. To measure for the cut tile at the finished end of the backsplash, hold a quarter-round where it will be set and mark its inside edge on the countertop tile **2**. Now place a field tile where it'll be set and transfer the pencil mark onto the tile **3**. Cut the tile to size and set it in place.

To lay the quarter-round trim, start on an outside corner of the splash with a "beak" (a quarter-round outside corner). You can lay the beak horizontally on top of the field tile **4** or stand it vertically **5**. If the beak is set vertically, you might need to trim its length to suit the height of the splash. To mark for this cut, first set a regular quarter-round atop the field tile, then hold a beak upside down and put a pencil mark even with

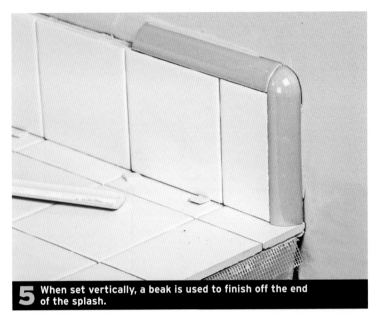

5 When set vertically, a beak is used to finish off the end of the splash.

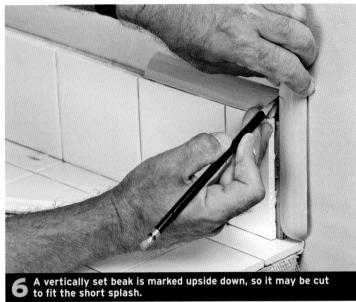

6 A vertically set beak is marked upside down, so it may be cut to fit the short splash.

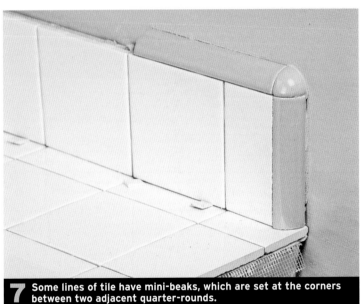

7 Some lines of tile have mini-beaks, which are set at the corners between two adjacent quarter-rounds.

8 Quarter-round trim tiles make a nice finish to a vintage-style backsplash on a kitchen counter.

the top of the quarter-round **6**. You can also finish off the corner with a "mini-beak," a trim piece available for some brands of tile. Set both the side and top quarter-round pieces first, then set the mini-beak flush and even with them **7**. Once the corner is finished, lay the rest of the quarter-rounds along the top of the splash, using your fingertips to make sure their ends are flush and even with each other **8**.

TRADE SECRET

If your tile installation has wide grout joints, use the same spacers used for the rest of the job to space the joints between individual trim pieces as well as between the trim and the field tile.

BACKSPLASH WITH DECORATIVE BORDER

1 Having all backsplash tiling materials close by makes for an easier installation.

2 Apply thinset carefully over any repaired and taped area of a wall.

3 Comb thinset on the wall in one direction, for best adhesion.

4 After setting the first row of tiles, use a level to check for straightness. Add wedges to adjust tile height as necessary.

5 A decorative strip of tiles is set above the first row of tile, and below the level of electrical boxes.

6 Insert wedges to help maintain an even grout joint.

Have all of your materials nearby for an efficient installation **1**. If you had to repair the wall to prep it for tile, spread the thinset carefully to avoid stripping off the fiberglass mesh tape **2**. Take care to comb the thinset thoroughly in one direction for better tile adhesion **3**.

Press the first row of tile in place, aligning the grout joints with the countertop tiles, if necessary. Level the row, adjusting individual tile height with wedges **4**. If your design includes decorative border tiles, set them in place carefully **5**, using wedges to adjust the tiles for even spacing and to create a properly sized grout joint between the border and the row of tiles below it **6**. Continue setting the remaining rows of field tiles above the border, pressing them firmly into the thinset **7**.

Cut and set tiles around electrical outlets and switches as necessary, leaving enough

7 Press each tile firmly into the wet thinset on the wall.

8 Use a pair of tile nippers to shape and rough up the otherwise sharp cut edge of a tumbled tile.

9 Round the edge of tumbled stone field tiles to make a nice clean finished edge.

10 The finished installation with geometric stone border tiles.

CUTTING IT SHORT

If you plan to use Decora®-type electrical fixtures, cut about two and a half threads of each screw off with an electrician's multicrimp and strip tool. This leaves the screws long enough to grab the electrical fixture but not strike the tile surface.

clearance for mounting screws and to allow for the metal ears of the switch or receptacle to rest on the tile. Cut the tiles for the backsplash's top row as needed and set them in place.

➡ See "Backsplash Layout," p. 137.

Because tumbled stone tiles like the ones used in this example often don't have available edge trim, you need to make your own trim tiles for the finished edges of the splash. After cutting edge tiles to size, round over and rough up the outside edge of each, using a pair of tile nippers **8**. The idea is to

make the cut edge look similar to a bull-nose edge **9**. The decorative border adds an interesting focal point in the finished backsplash **10**.

BACKSPLASH WITH DECOS

Another way to spruce up a basic backsplash is by interspersing some decorative (deco) tiles among the field tiles. This example shows a pattern of diagonally oriented deco tiles set in an alternating pattern across the backsplash. Decide on your layout before you begin.

➡ **See "Decorative Tiles," p. 125.**

You'll start setting tile from a plumb vertical line on the wall that's lined up with a grout joint in the center of your countertop ❶. After cutting field tiles as necessary to fit around the decos, spread thinset over the area on one side of the line and press the first tile firmly in place ❷. Continue setting cut and uncut tiles, as specified by your pattern, spreading more thinset as necessary for subsequent rows ❸. Use a beating block and hammer to embed the tiles into the thinset, making sure their faces are flush with one another. Use wedges under the first row of tiles to form an even joint between the backsplash and the countertop tile (you'll caulk this later). Continue inserting wedges between subsequent rows of tiles to hold them in place while the thinset dries ❹. If you need to tweak the position of tiles, try lifting them with a margin trowel, checking each row to make sure it's level ❺. Once a section of the splash is set with field tiles, set the decos in place while the thinset is still wet ❻. If the thinset has skinned over, scrape it off, back-butter the deco tile, and install it. Use wedges to adjust the position of each deco, so it's evenly spaced from the surrounding field tiles ❼, ❽. Continue spreading thinset and setting tile on the other side of the reference line.

If the splash will butt up to an upper cabinet or shelf, measure, cut, and install those tiles as you go. Be sure to leave a small gap between the top of the tiles and the cabinet for a caulk joint.

1 A plumb line drawn on the wall helps you line up the grout joints of the backsplash tiles with the tiles on the countertop.

2 Apply and comb thinset on one side of the plumb line and press tiles into place.

3 Continue setting both cut and whole tiles per your layout pattern, aligning them to the plumb line.

4 Use wedges to help maintain even grout joints between tiles and hold them in place until the thinset dries.

5 Check each row of tiles for level. Lift any low tiles with a margin trowel, then insert wedges to keep the tile in place.

6 Set the deco tiles into your backsplash while the thinset is still pliable.

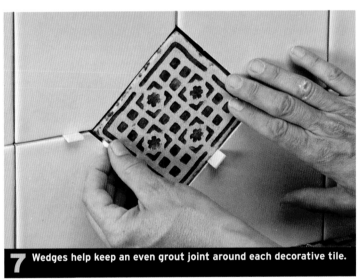

7 Wedges help keep an even grout joint around each decorative tile.

8 An alternating pattern of attractive deco tiles gives this backsplash nice visual interest.

TILING WAINSCOTING

1 Make a mark on the wall at the top measurement you've chosen for your wainscoting.

2 Use a level to make your mark into a continuous line for the new wainscoting.

In the 1950s, and even earlier, a tiled wainscoting was almost as commonplace as your toilet or vanity. And for good reason, since a wainscoting can serve practical purposes as well as aesthetic ones. A tiled wainscoting can offer protection for your walls or pedestal sink, add color or architectural elements, and even make an area seem larger by the expanse of tile. Tile walls are resistant to water and moisture so those areas will never need to be painted. Wainscoting lends lots of visual drama and ambiance to a bath or powder room, or to any wall you choose.

Before laying out the installation, you'll want to check the wall for any dramatically bowed areas and fill or flatten them as needed. The smoother the wall, the better the tile work will look, especially under overhead lighting.

➡ See "Backsplash Wall Repair and Prep," p. 120 and "Flattening the Wall," p. 121.

First, check your job site for outlets, switches, and windowsills to determine the height of the wainscoting that will work best. You might even wish to incorporate the backsplash into the wainscoting for a continuous line around the room. After you've determined this height, make a mark on the wall at that measurement **1**. You'll then use a level to draw a line all around the room **2**. This line will indicate the top of your tiled wainscoting.

Lay your tiles on a flat surface to lay out your design. Using the height of the wainscoting, measure from the top of your layout and make a mark on the field tile to represent the floor or bottom of the wainscoting **3**. Measure the distance from the top of the layout to the grout joint above this mark **4**. You'll use that measurement to set your first row of tile.

Return to the wall and measure down from the top line to make a mark at the bottom measurement **5**. Use a level and draw a line at this height **6**. Finally, find the halfway point on the wall and draw a vertical plumb line from the top line down to the floor **7**.

Next, you'll need a ledger board to hold up the tile. Screw any unwarped piece of wood or molding into the wall at the studs, keeping the top of the ledger board even with the bottom line **8**.

>> >> >>

3 Lay out your pattern and measure from the top trim tile down. Mark the tile that will be at the floor.

4 Note the measurement for the first grout joint above your bottom tile. This is where the ledger board will go.

5 Measure down from the top mark of your wainscoting to the grout joint above the bottom cut tile.

6 Make a level line across the wall at the grout joint to locate the ledger board.

7 From the top horizontal line, draw a line down the center of the wall to use as a reference.

8 Screw a ledger board into the wall studs at the bottom horizontal line.

TILING WAINSCOTING (CONTINUED)

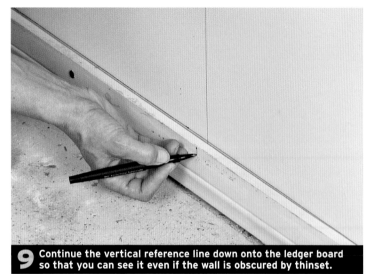

9 Continue the vertical reference line down onto the ledger board so that you can see it even if the wall is obscured by thinset.

10 Spread a manageable area with thinset above the ledger board.

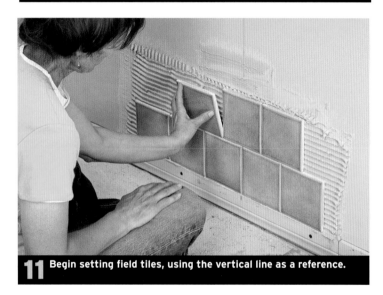

11 Begin setting field tiles, using the vertical line as a reference.

12 After you've set a couple of rows, check them with a level and adjust with spacers if necessary.

Then make a mark on the ledger board at the vertical reference line **9**. This line will serve as an additional guide after you spread thinset.

Spread and comb thinset over a small manageable area above the ledger board **10**. You'll begin setting tile, using the vertical line as a reference **11**. After setting a couple of rows, check the tiled rows for level **12**. Adjust with wedges as necessary. Continue tiling the wall with field tile, checking with the level every few rows **13**.

Comb the remaining area with thinset or back-butter individual decorative tiles, setting them in place **14**. Back-butter tile crown or top pieces as necessary **15**. Level the final row and use wedges to adjust **16**.

Leave the ledger board in place for 24 hours after you complete the wall. The next day, carefully remove the board. Measure and cut the bottom row of tiles to fit **17**. If the floor is out of level, these cuts will vary. Also, there's no need for perfection if a floor tile will cover the edge. If you're setting to a finished floor, take the extra care and leave space for a caulk joint. Allow the tile to set 24 hours and then grout. The finished wainscoting is shown in photo **18**.

➤ See "Applying Grout," p. 219.

13 Continue tiling up the wall, checking every few rows with a level, and adjusting with spacers.

14 Back-butter decorative tiles and set in place.

15 Back-butter the tile crown pieces and carefully squish into place.

16 Level the final row of tile and adjust with spacers.

17 The next day, remove the ledger board, cut your bottom row of tiles, and back-butter and set them, adjusting with spacers.

18 Tiled wainscoting with decorative relief tile and crown piece.

GROUTING, CAULKING & SEALING

G ROUTING, CAULKING, AND SEALING complete your tile, stone, or paver installation. Though these tasks come at the end, they actually have a most profound effect on the final look of your tile project as well as its durability and longevity. Although doing a good job of grouting may not seem as important as installing tile carefully, believe it or not, it's actually easier to hide a poor tile installation than an incompetent grout job. Poorly done tile jobs can be improved by well-executed grout; but the reverse, unfortunately, isn't the case.

BEFORE YOU BEGIN

Regardless of what kind of tile you've installed, the spaces between the tiles need to be filled with grout. Grout fills the space and smooths the transition between tiles, enhances the beauty of the tile, and makes it easier to keep the tiled surfaces clean. On some jobs, these spaces (called grout joints or lines) are very small. For example, some stone tiles, like granite and marble, nearly butt together, with only thin spaces (1/16 in. or less) between them. Other tiles, such as terra-cotta pavers, have large joints between the tiles–1/2 in., 3/4 in., or even wider.

The process starts with preparation to make the joints clean and regular. Then the grout is mixed to the correct consistency, applied to the tile, and forced into the open joints. The grout joints are then shaped to proper size and profile, and excess grout is wiped from the surface. Finally, the remaining dried grout residue is buffed off the tile, and the installation is ready for sealing and caulking. While the grouting process is virtually the same for almost all types of tile, there are special considerations for grouting some tile varieties, including glass, natural stone, and terra-cotta.

Preparing the installation space

If you've just laid your tile, you *must* allow the installation to dry at least 24 hours before you grout. The tile-setting adhesive needs to dry so that the tile is firmly bonded before grouting begins. If you don't wait for the adhesive to cure, the tiles may be knocked loose or out of position during grouting.

Make sure you have enough time to complete the grouting process from start to finish. If you have a large job, you can stop in an inconspicuous area and finish the job another day. However, it's preferable to enlist help to get all the grouting done in one go.

Grout can be quite sensitive to temperature: Excess heat makes grout dry too quickly and can cause cracking. Cold can delay the drying rate, possibly resulting in

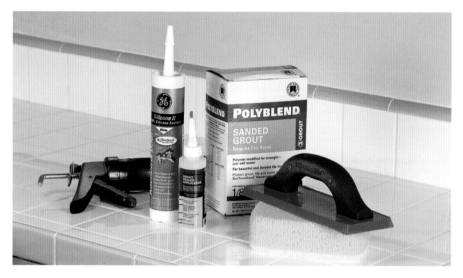

Be sure to assemble your tools and materials **before you begin. Some of the things you'll need are a grout float and large new sponges.**

efflorescence, a white haze that forms on the grout surface. Keep your work space, job site, the water used during grouting, and the grout itself at a temperature between 65°F and 75°F (and *never* apply heating or cooling air directly to drying grout). Place all your tools, grout materials, and even the water that you'll use for grouting in the room 24 hours before you begin, so that they'll all be the same temperature.

Preventing grout problems

To ensure dense, consistently colored joints on floors and countertops, always use water sparingly during the grouting process. Too wet a grout mix will likely cause weak, possibly powdery, and inconsistently colored grout joints. On walls, use a damp–but not a soaked or dripping–sponge for wipe down and never leave standing water on the tile or in the grout joints after cleanup.

Some factors that adversely affect grout cannot be controlled. Characteristics of some tiles, such as overglazing on the edges, or lugs, can cause uneven curing of the grout by allowing one joint to dry slower than another. Fortunately, these problems are usually invisible to all but the extremely discriminating eye.

New grout additives are now available **that make cement grouts much stronger and more impervious to stain. They are also easy to use as most are added with water or replace water entirely.**

WHAT CAN GO WRONG

Don't mix grout (or fill wipe-down buckets) with water run from a hot garden hose. Let the water run a while, until it cools.

CLEANING THE TILE

1 Long-nose pliers is a good tool for removing wedges.

2 Use both hands to steady the utility knife as you scrape thinset from between grout lines. A slip can scratch stone tiles.

3 Use the scrubbing side of a two-sided nonabrasive sponge to remove thinset and the soft side for cleaning.

Before you even think of opening that box or bag of grout, your first task is to make sure that all your grout joints are clean and free of debris and water. The last thing you want is an unsightly joint peppered with dirt and tile spacers or bits of mounting net and sponge. Remove any wedges and tile spacers used during tile installation with a pair of long-nose pliers or tile nippers **1**.

Use a razor knife to remove any excess adhesive or thinset from the edges of the tiles and from between the tiles **2**.

Cleaning excess thinset from the grout joints allows you to apply an even layer of material that will dry at a consistent cure rate. This helps make the grout not only stronger but more even in color as well. With a firm grip on your knife, carefully scrape each joint clean of excess material down to about two thirds of the thickness of the tile (for example, if the tile is $3/8$ in. thick, clean at least $1/4$ in. down into the joints). Make sure your knife's blade is sharp and change blades regularly because they wear down quickly. When working with tiles mounted to mesh netting, some stiff strands of mesh may be jutting out from the joints. Use the razor knife to cut these away from the tiles. Never twist the blade in a narrow joint, as you may accidentally chip the tile. When working with natural stone or very soft tile, take care to prevent the knife from slipping out of the grout joints and scratching the tile. Otherwise, you'll have the even bigger job of removing scratches or replacing tiles.

When all the joints are clean, wash the face of each tile thoroughly with a damp sponge **3**. If you have installed natural stone or porous tiles, this is the time to apply a sealer.

➡ See "Sealing Tile and Grout," p. 239.

WHAT CAN GO WRONG

If you accidentally scratch natural stone (honed or tumbled, not polished) during grouting, you can polish it out with a dampened piece of 400-grit wet/dry sandpaper. Use water as a lubricant and rub in a circular motion. If scratches on glazed tiles stand out, the tiles will, unfortunately, have to be removed and replaced.

CLEANING TEXTURED TILE

The word "textured" used to be used to describe a tile face that had more traction, or a tile that was slip resistant and safer for walking when it became wet. Today, "textured" has taken on a new meaning, and there's now a whole new variety of textured tiles, known more for their 3-D effect, varied smooth or rough features, beautiful undulations, unusual finish, and striking appearance. While these tiles produce a dramatic end result, they usually require some extra effort before grouting to ensure a truly polished and clean finish.

> **See "Textured and Graphic Tiles," pp. 24-25**

Before you grout, your tiles need to be as clean as possible. With most tiles, you'll keep the area fairly clean while you are working and wipe it down again before grouting. But between today's more resilient thinsets and the texture of the tiles, you may find that the texture requires a bit more effort to get the tiles clean. Residual film, left over from thinset, will cause the grout to cling, which results in streaking and leaves even more of a film or haze. While the haze can usually be cleaned later with an appropriate product, avoiding it in the first place is preferable.

Cleaning grout joints

Begin to clean by removing as much dried thinset from between the grout joints as possible with a utility knife. In some instances (especially if you have let the thinset cure for a day or more), you may want to use a Dremel®, a RotoZip®, or other rotary saw outfitted with a 1/16-in. to 1/8-in. diamond-impregnated bit. If you go this route, use a steady hand because it is easy to chip a tile edge or skitter out of the grout joint and scratch the tile face. If you are using rectified tile (see p. 39), you should also make sure that any thinset residue is removed from the side edges of the tile as even minor streaks of thinset at the top of the joint could show as a discolored line alongside the grout. You can also use a dry stiff scrub brush to clean these edges. Vacuum all of this loose material from inside the grout joints and off the surrounding floor.

When cured thinset is too hard, you may wish to use a rotary saw with a grout removal bit. Steady hands are a necessity!

Vacuum up all loose material from the joints and surrounding area.

Removing thinset haze

Always start with the mildest cleaning product available, and test a sample tile with any solution first. We recommend that you begin most cleaning with a high ph solution (available at most tile stores) or a diluted solution of vinegar and water (1/4 cup to 2 gal.).

Regardless of the cleaning solution, be sure to wear gloves and eye protection and wear protective or old clothing. After you've cleaned the joints, use a sponge dampened with the cleaning solution to clean thinset film off the surface of the tile. Then, wipe off the entire area using a clean sponge and a bucket of clean water. Be sure to remove any standing water from the face of the tile and out of the grout joints.

Allow the tiles to dry and if they appear clean (compare your tiles to a clean unused tile), you are good to grout. If the remaining residue is more stubborn, you may need to use a diluted solution of sulfamic acid (which may also be used for efflorescence, see p. 262) and water. You should mix and apply the acid in a well-ventilated area or set up a fan, if necessary. Follow the manufacturer's directions for dilution ratios, clean the area, and then wipe down the entire area again with fresh clean water. Always test on a spare tile to make sure the mild acid does not etch the finish.

Thinset haze or film **may cling tenaciously to the surface of textured tiles. An acidic solution may be necessary to remove it.**

Use a sponge or scrubber pad **to agitate the tile surface. Be sure to wipe down the entire surface with clean water afterward.**

This floor is clean **and ready to be grouted.**

MIXING GROUT

1 Always pour dry grout powder into the liquid, not vice-versa.

2 Mix grout completely, scraping the sides and bottom of the bucket.

3 You can add water to a too-dry grout mix a little at a time by squeezing it from a sponge.

The bucket in the middle **has the correct consistency. The grout on the left is too dry. The pourable grout on the right will dry to a weak powdery joint.**

It's best to mix a small amount of grout at first and learn to become consistent at preparing the material to the proper consistency. Grout goes off and become unworkable in only a few hours—less in hot weather.

You'll need a small, clean bucket and a margin trowel for mixing the grout powder and water together. Follow the manufacturer's instructions for mixing the powder with either water and water with a latex additive.

➤ See "Choosing Grout," pp. 84–86.

Start with less liquid than you think you need, adding the grout powder ❶ to the bucket and mixing it thoroughly with a margin trowel ❷. For really big batches, use a power mixer.

➤ See "Mixing Thinset," p. 81.

Gradually add more liquid as necessary by squeezing it from a clean sponge ❸.

Keep stirring until the grout is thoroughly mixed, with no puddles of water or pockets of unmixed powder. Ideally, the final mix should have a soft, but not slushy, consistency that resembles peanut butter or toothpaste. The grout should have a sheen but not be too shiny or wet looking.

After mixing, allow the grout to slake for 10 minutes (or according to the directions on the bag). Slaking is a physical and chemical reaction that allows the liquid to penetrate and dissolve all of the components of the grout. It's very important to allow this rest period because slaking directly affects the final density, shading, and color of the grout. After slaking, stir the grout thoroughly without adding any additional liquid. The mixture may seem stiff at first, but adding liquid will weaken the grout.

WHAT CAN GO WRONG

Never dip a wet margin trowel or gloved hand into a box or bag of grout, as you'll cause clumps in the powder.

APPLYING GROUT

1 Margin trowels work well for scooping grout from the bucket to load the grout float.

2 Spread grout firmly across the tile with the grout float. Use a low angle and fully pack the joints.

3 Be sure to fill the sides and the edges of tile with grout.

4 Remove excess grout by holding the rubber float at a sharp angle to the tile. Move diagonally to the joint.

Grout only a small area at a time. Plan on working a space you can cover in 10 minutes: about 3 lin. ft. or less of a kitchen backsplash or 50 sq. ft. of a bathroom floor. As your experience grows, you can do larger areas, but in the beginning, pace yourself.

Start by putting a margin trowel full of grout mixture on your float **1** (or scoop it up with the float itself) and spread it across the tile. Hold the rubber part of the float at a low angle relative to the tile as you pack the grout into the joints. Move the float diagonally across the tile **2** and don't be afraid to push the grout into those joints or to go over an area more than once. You can use either the long or the short end of the float to work grout into joints between trim tiles and at the edges of your tile installation **3**.

At this point, don't worry about how the grout joints look or about leaving excess grout behind. Just be sure that you have fully packed all joints, except the joints that will be caulked later.

After the joints in your work area are filled, clean the face of your grout float with a damp sponge. Now, angle the float at 45° relative to the face of the tile and sweep it diagonally across the surface to remove the excess grout **4**. Move the float along diagonally to prevent its edge from denting or digging into the wet grout joints. Don't be too fanatical, but the more grout you remove from the tile's surface with the float, the easier your final wipe down will be.

> ⚠ **WARNING**
> Always wear rubber gloves and work clothes when you work with grout. The alkaline nature of this stuff severely dries skin and can even cause fingertips to bleed.

WIPE DOWN

Once grout has been applied to the joints over a manageable area of your tile installation ❶, you're ready to wipe the excess from the face of the tiles and shape the joints. Shaping enhances the beauty of the tile by forming pleasing, uniform grout lines. It isn't a difficult process, but it's important to wipe down and shape at the right time: Act too soon, and you may wipe the grout right out of the joint; too late, and there'll be lots of extra work removing hardened grout from the face of the tile. Waiting 15 minutes to 30 minutes after grouting is complete is usually about right for average ceramic tile in a 65°F to 75°F room. Watch for evidence of grout drying on the face of the tile or the grout turning a slightly lighter color. Also, try touching a grout joint lightly with the tip of your finger. It should be just firm, leaving only a slight impression. Wiping and shaping only a small area at a time makes it easier to gauge your timing as you work and discover how long each step takes. Your timing will improve as you move on to each new section.

To begin the wiping and shaping process, immerse a sponge in a bucket of cool, clean water. Squeeze the sponge out until it is just damp—no dripping water (remember, excess water is an enemy of grout). Begin with a light touch and start wiping the tile with a circular or diagonal motion. Do not wipe parallel to the joints as this will remove too much grout ❷.

Rinse your sponge frequently, especially when you see its pores filling with grout. The idea is to clean the excess grout from the face of the tile and begin shaping the joints to make them look uniform; not too wide or too narrow. With most tiles, a slightly concave grout joint relative to the face of the tile is correct. If you find a void, hole, or indentation, fill it with a bit of grout ❸.

1 Grout joints should be filled and tile surfaces clean.

2 Wipe diagonally across tiles with a well-squeezed sponge to remove excess grout.

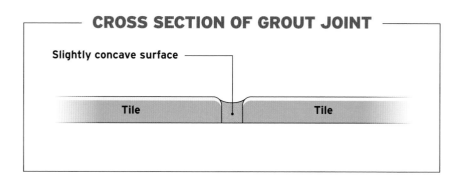

3 Check for areas of missing grout, especially around relief tiles. Fill with a fingertip full of grout.

CROSS SECTION OF GROUT JOINT

Slightly concave surface

| Tile | | Tile |

JOINT SHAPING

After you've grouted and wiped down one area, you'll get a better sense of the timing required for the process. Continue grouting small, manageable areas of your tile installation, following a routine of applying grout, wiping down, shaping the joints, and then moving on to the next area. To save time, apply grout to the next area before wiping down the previous one. This gives the grout in the new section enough setup time, yet allows you to blend the joints of the freshly shaped grout with areas previously completed.

Once your entire installation has been grouted and shaped, check the corners and edges of the tile (for example, where backsplashes meet or the joint between the backsplash and the counter) ❶ for pockets of excess grout and clean them out with your razor knife as necessary. You will caulk these areas later. Examine all walls and woodwork adjacent to the tile installation and wipe off any grout that has ended up on these surfaces ❷. Wherever trim butts up to walls or cabinets, use a screwdriver or chisel to scrape the grout from the edge of the tiles making the grout flat and smooth ❸. Run a dampened sponge or finger over these joints, to smooth them out ❹. Once all the tile has been wiped and shaped, rinse your sponge, dampen it, and run it diagonally across the entire installation once again. With big tiles (8 in. sq. or larger), you may wipe just the face of each tile and leave the shaped grout joints alone. With smaller tiles, it may be too difficult to do this, so just wipe with a light touch. This time, the tile faces should look almost completely clean and the joints should be crisp and consistent. Don't worry about leaving light grout residue on the faces of the tiles.

1 Clean any grout out from the joint between the backsplash and counter tiles with a utility knife.

2 Sponge and smooth grout that may have collected in the joint on top of the tiles. Sponge excess grout off the walls.

3 A screwdriver or chisel can be used to carve any excess grout from the top edge of tiles.

4 Sponge areas to make them smooth and for touch ups.

FINAL CLEANUP

1 Remove any light grout haze from tile surface with a clean, dry cheesecloth.

2 Polishing with cheesecloth restores the luster of the tile.

3 The finished installation.

After the tile is clean, allow any grout residue on the tile surface to dry naturally, leaving a light film or haze. Depending on conditions, this may take from 10 minutes to up to 2 hours. If you're polishing up a new floor, wide joints may stay somewhat wet and malleable for days after grouting. As much as possible, avoid walking on the joints when you polish. Polish or buff off the light grout haze with a dry cheesecloth or soft, lint-free white cloth **❶**.

Be sure to wear a dust mask or other breathing protection for this procedure as the silica dust that is kicked up is harmful to your lungs. Keep an eye out for small pinholes or imperfections in the grout and for joints you may have dented or dinged. If you spot one, touch it up with a dab of grout and polish it very lightly. Again, use a light touch overall and take care not to change the shape of the grout joints. The tile itself will return to its natural luster after wiping **❷**.

You must allow the grout joints to cure before the tile is ready for use. Curing is the chemical process during which grout gains strength and density. During curing, grout is vulnerable and porous. Full

curing can take up to 6 months or more. But fortunately, most types of grout cure enough in 2 days to 3 days to make tile surfaces usable and floors ready to walk on.

It's important to let the grout joints dry naturally, ideally at a moderate room temperature (64°F to 75°F). *Do not* attempt to artificially dry the tile with the a fan, blow dryer, or portable heater. If you accelerate the drying process, the water that's necessary for curing evaporates too quickly, resulting in weak or cracked grout joints.

If you have the time and patience, you can actually make your grout significantly stronger by keeping it moist for the first few days after application. Slowing the curing process this way makes a huge difference in the density and ease of future cleaning of the grout. Use a damp sponge or mop to moisten the joints once a day for 2 days or 3 days, starting 24 hours after you complete grouting. Use just enough water to darken the joint but do not leave standing water.

A successful grout job has even color and joints filled to the same depth **❸**.

EPOXY GROUTING

Since we wrote the previous edition of this book, epoxy grout has become more user-friendly and is now a great alternative to cement grouts. The big plus with epoxy grout is that it is extremely stain resistant (some brands actually claim to be stainproof), provides consistent color, doesn't shrink (which means less possible hairline cracking), and is dust-free.

There are some differences between installing tile with epoxy grout and with cement grout, but it is an easy transition if you follow the instructions carefully. Also, if you need to do a repair in an installation that has epoxy grout, we'll show you how to do that in the "Maintenance & Repair" chapter, starting on p. 242.

Epoxy grout systems are made up of two (or three) parts. There is a resin and the activator (often with colorant, though that may be packaged separately) that alters the two parts into a hardened formula. Some brands have a stronger chemical odor than others.

Working with epoxy grout

Before you begin, it's important to read the manufacturer's directions/specifications because you have less open time with epoxy than with cement grout. Working with epoxy grout is a timed process and if it gets away from you, it may be difficult to fix any issues. For your first installation, plan on spreading an area no larger than you think you can comfortably grout in 20 minutes. It's always better to be safe than sorry for your first go around.

Also before you begin to mix or spread the grout, have all of your tools ready to go: gloves, epoxy float, sponges, white scrub pads, microfiber towels, and buckets filled with water (with cleaning additive provided by the manufacturer or recommended by them). You won't have time to gather them once you've begun the process. You should also wear your least favorite clothes or work clothes. Epoxy grout is not the least bit forgiving, and it's the gift that keeps on

>> >> >>

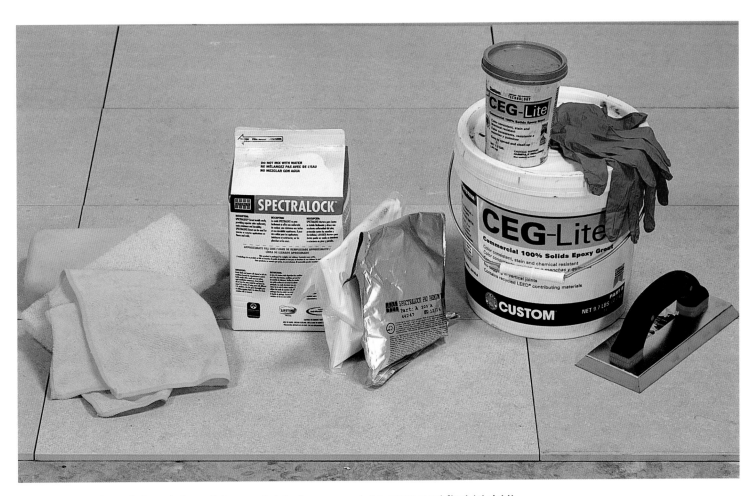

Have all your tools ready to go before mixing up a batch of epoxy grout. An epoxy grout float (at right) is harder and heavier than a standard float and nonporous to resist gumming up from the epoxy.

EPOXY GROUTING (CONTINUED)

1 Stir each of your epoxy components (the hardener and the resin) until you have a homogenous mix.

2 Pour and/or combine components into one container.

3 Mix grout components together until the color is consistent.

4 Scoop the mixture onto waterproof paper or a board.

giving if you do get it on your clothing. It adheres beautifully and is tenacious.

Choose a mixing area with ventilation and be sure to mix on something disposable in case of a spill. To begin, thoroughly mix all parts separately before mixing them together ❶. Then combine all parts until you have a homogenous mix ❷, ❸. Dump the mixed epoxy onto a piece of waterproof paper, board, or other open surface that you can easily move around ❹.

If you leave epoxy in your mixing bucket, it will set up too quickly. Spread the grout into the joints with your epoxy grout float, but be sure to remove as much as possible from the face of the tiles ❺.

➡ See "Applying Grout," p. 219.

After spreading a manageable area of wall or floor, check the time. Depending on the particular grout company, you may start wiping immediately or per their instructions ❻. Fill any voids or pin holes at this time ❼. Do not exceed the recommended time allotment. Epoxy grout has the opposite need of cement grout: With cement grout, water is the enemy but with epoxy grout, water is a good friend. Don't wring your sponge out but instead, allow water to aid you when you wipe down the surface. If you don't use enough water, you will pull grout from the joints instead of shaping them. But you also must take care to keep water out of the ungrouted joints. Your sponge will also not last as long as with cement grouts. The pores will clog with epoxy stickiness and become unusable, so be sure to have additional sponges on hand.

5 Use an epoxy float to fill the grout joints fully but be sure to remove any excess grout from the face of the tile.

TRADE SECRET

If you are wiping floor grout, you will need to protect your knee pads by wrapping them with waterproof paper. If you do not, the sticky residue on your pad will pull the epoxy out of the grout joints as you go over the grouted areas.

6 Shape the joints with a wet sponge and clean the face of the tile. Use plenty of water.

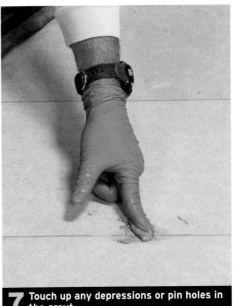

7 Touch up any depressions or pin holes in the grout.

EPOXY GROUTING (CONTINUED)

8 Agitate the surface of the tile with a white scrub pad and it will loosen any residual grout. Use care to prevent gouging your shaped grout joints.

9 Any water on the tile will contain grout residue. Drag a damp microfiber towel diagonally across the tile to remove any excess water.

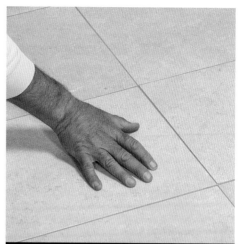

10 Feel the face of the tiles with your bare hands to locate any grout residue. If you feel any stickiness or granules, wipe them off.

For your second wipe down, wait the prescribed amount of time, then use a white scrubber pad with clean water to agitate the surface of the tiles to loosen any epoxy residue before you use a microfiber cloth **8**. If you are wiping a floor, remember to flip your kneepad to a clean side or protect it again or you'll be pulling and dragging epoxy grout around the floor. To use your microfiber cloth, wring it out thoroughly before each diagonal pass over a tile **9**. Keep in mind that any remaining water will contain epoxy residue, so you want to use your cloth to remove as much water as possible. For a larger area (over 50 sq. ft.), you will need to clean out your water bucket periodically. With bare hands, feel the surface of the tile for any epoxy residue and wipe again if necessary **10**.

If you did not complete grouting the entire area at one time, proceed as described earlier with a new unit of epoxy grout and continue on from wherever you left off. The following day, inspect the grouted area and if you find a small bit of residue, use a paint scraper to remove it **11**. If you find epoxy film on the surface, you can use an epoxy haze remover **12**.

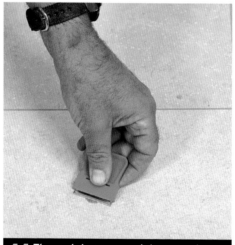

11 The next day, use a paint scraper to easily remove any grout from the surface of the tile.

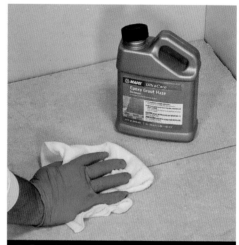

12 Additionally, wipe any remaining epoxy film off the surface with epoxy haze remover.

TRADE SECRET

Unlike working with cement grout, after epoxy grout has cured (hours or days later) you can blend in a new unit of epoxy grout without any color or texture issues.

COUNTER EDGES

1 Always check the front edges for thinset and clean well with a damp sponge.

2 Use a sharp utility knife to remove excess thinset.

3 Put a small amount of grout on the end of your float and fill the joints.

4 Push the grout-filled margin trowel under the front edge tiles.

5 Use a sharp razor knife to trim excess grout from the lower edge of the trim tiles.

6 Cut off the protective tape and paper below the tiles with a utility knife.

Counter edges require a slightly different grouting process than flat countertops and floors, one that demands a bit more attention to detail. First, clean the front edge tiles with a sponge and carefully clean out the joints with a razor knife ❶. Be sure to also use the knife to clean the edges underneath the front edge of the tiles ❷.

➡ See "Cleaning the Tile," p. 215.

After grouting the counter surface, fill in the front edge tiles with grout applied with the short edge of the float ❸. Then use a margin trowel to fill in the gap between the cabinet face and the edge tile ❹. This extra step gives your job a professional appearance and makes the underside of the counter feel smooth and continuous. On bar tops and other overhanging tile counters, finishing the underside prevents rough tile and grout from snagging clothing and scratching skin. Once the grout has dried, use a fresh blade in the razor knife to cut away the excess grout ❺ and the protective paper on your cabinets ❻.

GLASS TILE

Unlike regular glazed ceramic tiles, glass tiles require a little bit different procedure for grouting. Start by cleaning the joints with a razor knife as usual **1**.

➡ See "Cleaning the Tile," p. 215.

Use a firm-bristle toothbrush to finish cleaning the narrow joints between small mosaic tiles **2**. Work gently, but don't be alarmed if some tiles pop off during the cleaning process. Just clean the tile by scraping off the thinset from both the back of the tile and from the substrate where the tile popped off. Back-butter the tile with fresh thinset and press it back into place. Clean the entire tile surface with a damp sponge **3**.

➡ See "Replacing a Tile," facing page.

When applying grout—especially sanded grout—to glass tile, always exercise great caution so as not to scratch the tile (some manufacturers specify nonsanded or sanded grout for their tile, so be sure to check before purchasing). Use a slightly wetter grout mixture than usual and apply it with a soft rubber float that's specifically designed for use with glass **4**. Use a light touch as you apply and spread the grout. If you have any newly reset tiles, it's best to first grout around them with a gloved finger, and then grout around them with the float.

Since glass is nonporous and set on an antifracture membrane that limits water absorption, grout will take much longer to set up in the joints of a glass tile installation. Therefore, you must be patient and allow more time before wiping down the grout. Instead of 10 minutes, you might wait up to 30 minutes, checking the joint periodically for firmness. Use a soft sponge and wipe down and shape joints much as you would for ceramic tiles **5**. After shaping, let the tile dry until a haze forms, then wipe the glass clean with cheesecloth **6**.

⚠ WARNING

Frosted, sandblasted, and/or specially treated glass tiles may need to be sealed before grouting. Always refer to the manufacturer's instructions when using these tiles.

1 Clean thinset from between small joints with a utility knife or a toothbrush.

2 The bristles on a firm toothbrush work well to clean joints between glass tiles.

3 Clean glass tile with the soft foam side of a sponge.

4 Apply the grout, then remove as much grout as possible from the face of the glass mosaics with a low-angled grout float.

5 Wipe the excess grout from the glass tiles.

6 Polish off any grout haze from the glass tiles to leave a shimmering surface.

Replacing a Tile

Don't be alarmed if a mosaic tile pops off while you're cleaning.

Clean the tile by scraping off the thinset with a utility knife.

Using a small margin tool, back-butter the tile with fresh thinset.

Reset the tile back in its place. Remember its location when you start to grout.

NATURAL STONE

Some stone tiles, especially travertine, are full of holes and surface cavities. You may love the open, rustic look of these nooks and crannies, favor the smoother appearance of the stone's surface filled with grout, or prefer a look that's halfway in between. First, always seal natural stone. Next, to achieve the rustic look, simply tape off the surfaces of the tiles with blue tape before sealing and grouting ❶. If you prefer the smooth, filled look, simply grout after sealing.

> **See "Sealing Natural Stone," p. 241.**

Spread the grout as usual, taking care to ensure that the bigger craters in the tiles are fully filled.

For the in between look, tape off only the holes and cavities that you wish to leave open and not fill with grout (it is better to tape off more holes at first, as you can always grout them in later if the tile looks too rustic). Spread the grout over your taped or untaped stone ❷ and wipe down, leaving the blue tape intact. Allow the grout to dry, polish the overall surface, then remove the tape ❸. Finally, polish off any remaining haze from the previously taped areas.

For natural stone that's partially filled, the tile surface should appear clean. Grout joints will be shaped and full but should not appear wet.

The texture and features of natural stone are visible and ungrouted.

1 Use masking or blue tape on tiles to prevent grout from filling holes.

2 Grout over taped areas with care.

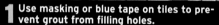

3 Remove tape to expose the holes and texture of natural stone.

PORCELAIN TILE

Porcelain tiles absorb water very slowly, which allows grout to set up on the face of the tile while it's still soft in the grout joints. If you wait for the joints to set up, as you would with regular ceramic tile, the grout dries on the porcelain and is difficult to clean off. Therefore, you must wipe down porcelain tiles and shape the joints while the grout is still wet and soft ❶. This requires a deft touch. First, wait for 10 minutes to 20 minutes, then shape the joints very carefully, wiping and cleaning the surface with great care ❷. The grout will take much longer to cure in porcelain tile than standard tile, and in some rare situations, you may see some efflorescence, which looks like a white powder atop the grout. Clean this off, as described on p. 262.

1 Porcelain tiles will have a fully hazed (lighter in color) surface while the grout in the joints is still soft (and dark in color).

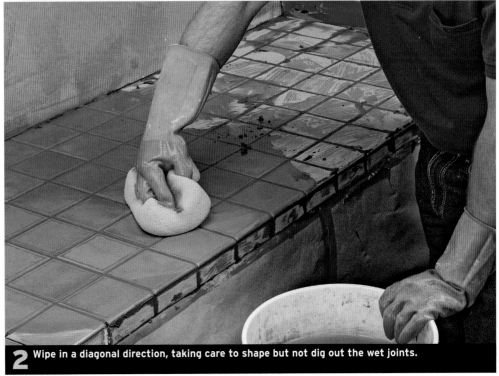

2 Wipe in a diagonal direction, taking care to shape but not dig out the wet joints.

DECORATIVE TILE

Glazed decorative or relief tiles with embossed elements are a beautiful addition to any tile job. Unfortunately, those beautiful raised elements tend to hold grout, which can muddy the look of decorative tiles. Keeping grout out of the recesses will save hours of work trying to clean them up later. Here is a method that works for us: After all the grout joints are clean and the tile is dry, tape off the embossed areas with blue masking tape ❶. Work your way around each deco tile until the entire face is covered to the edges ❷. Be accurate with your taping, since the grout will cling to every uncovered portion of the tile. Now grout the tiles as normal ❸. After the final wipe down and polishing, peel the tape off ❹ and use your fingertip to touch up any joints that may have been pulled off by the edge of the tape ❺. The tile surface remains clean ❻.

TRADE SECRET
Remember to use a damp, not dripping, sponge to wipe down the tiles.

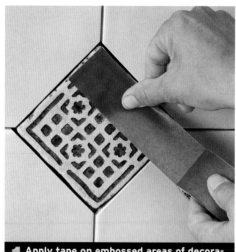

1 Apply tape on embossed areas of decorative tile to keep grout out of the design.

2 Taped embossed tile will remain free from grout when the area is grouted.

3 Grout as usual. Use care and avoid dislodging the tape.

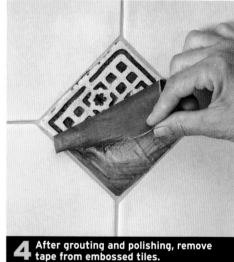

4 After grouting and polishing, remove tape from embossed tiles.

5 Touch up any edge voids or holes with a dab of grout.

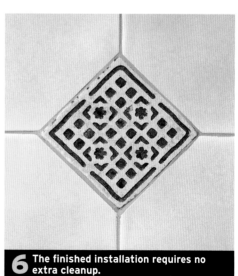

6 The finished installation requires no extra cleanup.

TERRA-COTTA PAVERS

Unlike other types of tile, terra-cotta pavers, such as Saltillos, have idiosyncrasies that require a little special attention come grouting time. To accommodate their irregular nature, it's best to set them with larger grout joints than you'd use with most tiles. For joints up to 1/2 in. wide, you can use regular sanded grout. But big pavers with joints up to 1 in. wide require a special grout mix called Saltillo grout. This is because terra-cotta tiles absorb moisture from grout as it dries, which will cause regular sanded grout to crack. Commercially made Saltillo grout typically comes in two colors: gray and tan; but you can mix your own custom color if you wish.

Before grouting, you must clean the grout joints, as always. But be extra careful with pavers, because one slip with the razor knife can lead to a deep scratch and a tile that must be replaced ❶. All paver tiles must be sealed before grouting ❷. The sealer prevents the grout color from moving into the faces of the pavers and slows down moisture absorption from the grout. Make sure the sealer is dry before going on to the next step.

➤ See "Sealing Tile and Grout," p. 239.

Wide grout joints between pavers require lots of grout, so you'll need to mix a fairly large quantity to cover even a modest area of floor. While your grout is slaking, dampen the tiles with water. This helps slow down the setting up of the grout and makes grouting easier. For smaller areas, use a sponge and water and wipe the tiles down ❸. Mist larger areas using a pump sprayer, like the kind used for misting indoor plants. For really big floors, use a garden hose fitted with a mist nozzle. Don't leave any standing water, just dampen all tiles and grout joints. >> >> >>

TRADE SECRET

If you are grouting more than 100 sq. ft. of paver tiles, have extra sponges on hand. Sponges shred and wear out quickly, and you don't want to have to pick bits of sponge out of the grout.

1 Take care to not scratch the pavers when you are cleaning the joints.

2 Apply sealer with a clean cloth in one direction to cover the tiles.

3 Dampen the installation with a clean sponge before grouting.

TERRA-COTTA PAVERS (CONTINUED)

4 Put a good amount of grout on the floor to start. These are big grout joints.

5 Force grout into the joints with the short end of the grout float.

6 Work in a diagonal direction.

7 Wipe and shape the grout joints with a sponge.

8 Strong arms are handy for squeezing grout from the bag.

Using a grout float

There are two ways to apply grout in the large quantities needed to fill wide joints.

The first method is to transfer handfuls of grout to the tile, then use a grout float to spread it into the joints **4**, **5**. You need to spread a lot of material with the float, but big joints are easier to grout than narrow ones, so this way of working isn't all that bad. It's advisable to work an area no bigger than what you can cover in 5 minutes. Once the joints in the work area are filled, hold the float at an angle and sweep across the tile diagonally to remove excess grout **6**. Use the sponge to shape the joints and wipe off excess residue as with smaller tiles **7**. Since grout sets up fast on pavers, don't let it dry too much before you wipe down. Work your way across the floor from one corner of the room to a doorway where you can exit the room without tracking back across the tile.

Using a grout bag

The other way to grout pavers is what we call the "arm-buster" method. It requires a special grout bag, which looks like a really big pastry bag you'd use to decorate a cake. Although it's difficult to master, the grout bag lets you grout large joints quickly. Fill the bag with a grout mixture that's wetter than usual (so it will squeeze out easily), then fold the end of the bag over. Squeeze the bag to dispense grout directly into the joints **8**. Work your way down each joint, filling it until it overflows slightly. If you are working by yourself, do an area of about 4 sq. ft. to start. Now put the bag aside and use a margin trowel as a spatula to press and firmly compact grout into each joint **9**. Then use the edge of the trowel to slice off excess material **10**. As always, if you see a spot you missed, fill it with a blob of grout **11**. Since grout sets up quickly on terra-cotta tiles, wipe down may begin soon after the grout has been applied. As before, use your sponge to first shape the joints to a uniform look. Then do a final wipe down to remove as much grout residue from the face as possible **12**. Wait a few hours, then use clean rags, towels, or cheesecloth to remove any surface hazing. It's also normal to end up with a fair amount of loose sand that has separated out of the grout. Vacuum the sand off the tiles or sweep it up with a soft-bristle brush.

The finished grout job should have consistent joints **13**.

9 Compact the grout in each joint with the end of the margin trowel.

10 Remove any excess grout material with the margin trowel.

11 Fill any holes or low spots with excess grout.

12 Clean the faces of the tiles without disturbing the grout joints. Clean as well as you can so that final cleanup will be minimal.

13 Nice work! Uniform, consistent grout joints.

Working with black grout

Grouting with black grout can add a classy look to your tile job. Unfortunately, the pigment that makes black grout black stains pretty much everything it touches. Before you begin, tape off all walls, baseboards, trim, and anything that might possibly make contact with the grout. Always mix black grout in a clean container or pail that's expendable after the job's done. Don two pairs of gloves for grouting: An inner pair of latex or Nitrile® gloves, covered by an oversize pair of rubber gloves. Double gloving not only protects your hands from stains but allows you to pull off an outer glove to do the occasional touchup without getting black fingertips. Wear at least a single pair of gloves when polishing tiles with a cheesecloth to prevent the black haze from ending up on your hands. Keep your grouting tools from touching anything until you've cleaned them thoroughly with lots of water.

APPLYING CAULK

Caulking creates a pliable, waterproof joint between adjacent sections of tile or between different materials, like granite and ceramic tile. This flexible seam is necessary because of the slight movement between surfaces: backsplashes and counters, walls and floors, and so on. Even slight movement can cause grout (an inflexible material) to crack around sinks or between tiled backsplashes and granite counters. Movement that causes substrate under the tile to move can even cause cracks in the tile itself. Tiles can expand and contract, which is why, for example, it's imperative to caulk all seams between glass-tiled surfaces and surrounding materials.

The caulking material used for most tile jobs is a flexible, waterproof product that's silicone based. You can buy caulks in a wide variety of textures and colors, allowing you to choose caulk that matches both the color and texture of the grout you've used.

➡ See "Caulk," p. 88.

Basic application method

Use a squeeze tube of caulk for small projects, but for medium and larger jobs, a caulk cartridge applied with a caulk gun is the best choice. To achieve a good-looking caulking job, you must use the gun properly. To load the gun, press and hold the plunger release button with your thumb, pull the plunger back, then slip the caulk tube in place. Push the plunger in until it contacts the inside of the cartridge and take your thumb off the release. Now cut the tip of the caulk cartridge at a slight angle with your utility knife ❶. Cut near the tip, to create a small opening; you can always enlarge the opening later, if necessary. Some caulk tubes have an inner seal where the tip joins the tube. Use a small stick or large nail to break the seal.

Before you tackle the tile, practice running a bead of caulk on a piece of cardboard or scrap wood. When you're ready to caulk, squeeze the gun's trigger gently and move the tip of the tube along the grout joint steadily to lay down a continuous, even bead ❷. It is better to use less caulk and add more on a second pass than to apply too much. After finishing a section, use a dampened finger to smooth the caulk bead along the joint ❸. It's best to run a bead that's about 5 ft. long or less at a time, then smooth that section before starting on the next. After smoothing, take a small, damp sponge and bend it in half in your hand ❹. Run the sponge along the joint line to do a little final smoothing and to clean any remaining caulk residue from the tile and/or counter surface ❺. The final caulk joint should be about the same size as a grout joint. If it is too small, immediately add caulk sparingly and smooth the joint again. If the joint is too large, use a paper towel to remove the excess caulk, then smooth again. Make all repairs to your caulk joints immediately. Otherwise, the caulk will skin over and you will have to scrap it all off and start over.

Caulking is especially important at joints where there will be water, such as sinks and bathtubs.

1 Slice off the tip of the caulk tube at an angle. Cut it near the top of the tube to ensure a small opening.

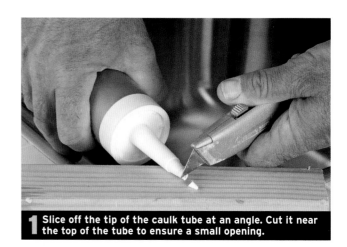

2 Move steadily along the grout joint as you apply a continuous, smooth bead of caulk.

CAULKING AROUND SINKS

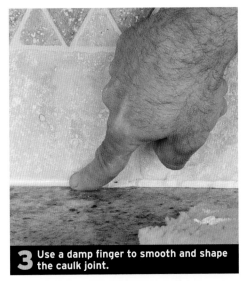

3 Use a damp finger to smooth and shape the caulk joint.

4 Use a damp folded sponge to smooth the joint and remove excess caulk.

5 Use a damp noncellulose or shed-free sponge to remove caulk residue.

1 A clean, smooth corner where two beads of caulk intersect.

2 Before caulking, remove excess thin-set between the trim and the sink.

3 Use caulk matched to the grout.

4 A clean finger will smooth a corner joint.

In addition to sealing seams between walls, backsplashes, and floors, caulk is the ideal material to create a clean waterproof seal between a sink (or plumbing fixtures) and the tile surrounding it **1**. Whether made of metal, porcelain, or other material, sinks expand and contract at a different rate from the surrounding tile. Hence, you should always add a flexible caulk joint around a sink before installing plumbing fixtures, to prevent cracks between the sink and the tile.

Start by using a razor knife to clean out any grout that's present in the joint between the tile and the sink **2**.

▶ See "Removing Grout," p. 249.

Now run a bead of caulk where the tile and the sink meet, around the entire perimeter **3**. Smooth the bead and clean off any excess caulk. If your sink has square corners, use a dampened finger to push the caulk bead into each corner and then smooth it out **4**.

EXPANSION JOINTS IN TILE FLOORS

To allow a tile floor to expand and contract and prevent the problems movement can cause, you must add expansion joints between sections of tile. Expansion joints are spaces filled with flexible caulk that allows movement. On large floors, tile industry standards call for an expansion joint every 24 ft. to 36 ft.

On floors that are smaller than this, it's adequate to leave a space wherever the floor meets a wall, column, or other obstacle. This expansion joint is no less than ¼ in. to ½ in. wide, and must be figured in when laying out and setting the tile.

Before caulking expansion joints, you must protect adjacent tiles by covering them with kraft paper taped in place ❶. Vacuum out any debris so that all joints are clean ❷. If expansion joints are ½ in. deep or more, install a strip of flexible foam material to reduce the amount of caulking you need to apply.

➡ See "Caulk," p. 88.

Push the strip down into all the joints around the floor, using a margin trowel or other tool to make sure it seats firmly and doesn't stick up above the tile surface ❸. Apply the caulk into the joint over the foam, making sure it fills up to the top of the tile ❹. On wide joints, you may have to apply the bead in two passes. Often, the joint will be covered by baseboard when the floor is completed. But if the joint will show, use a moistened finger to smooth the caulk and touch up as necessary ❺. As soon as you are finished caulking along one wall, pull up the tape and paper before the caulk has a chance to dry and stick to the tape ❻.

1 Before caulking a floor, use blue tape and paper to protect the perimeter.

2 Vacuum out any debris from the joint before caulking.

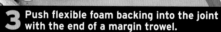
3 Push flexible foam backing into the joint with the end of a margin trowel.

4 Caulk the joint, making sure that it is filled.

5 Smooth the joint with a dampened finger and touch up if necessary.

6 Remove the tape and paper before the caulk dries.

SEALING TILE AND GROUT

Sealers for tile and grout perform slightly different functions but are each indispensable for a quality, long-lasting tile installation. Sealers protect porous tile, such as terra-cotta, and grout from the cold (or hot) cruel world of spilled coffee, red wine, grape juice, and other food. Sealers are not a cure-all but rather a preventative measure. For example, if you drip hot coffee across the counter, a good sealer will allow the drip to bead up until you sponge it away. But even the best sealer won't keep food spills left to dry from permanently staining your tile job.

Sealing tile

While glazed or high-fired tiles generally do not require sealing, unglazed tiles, crackle-glazed tiles, and stone tiles must be sealed before grouting to prevent color in the grout staining the tile. The best way to seal the tile is to coat it with a penetrating sealer (also known as an "impregnator").

See "Sealers," p. 87.

The exception is paver tiles, which require a special finish involving multiple coats.

See "Terra-Cotta Pavers," p. 233.

The only tools you need for the sealing process are a small plastic bucket, a clean sponge or lint-free cloth, a pair of rubber gloves, and—if you're sealing a floor—kneepads. Most sealers we recommend are water based and safe and easy to use for home tile installations. If you choose a solvent-based sealer, you must wear breathing protection.

Begin by pouring a small quantity of sealer into your bucket. A little goes a long way and you can always refill the bucket. Dip your sponge or cloth into the sealer and wring it out, leaving it wet but not dripping. Start applying the sealer to the farthest corner of your tile job and work your way out. Wipe the sealer onto the faces of the tiles, striving to apply an even coat. Cover each tile completely, but try not to get any into the grout joints. Don't be overly concerned if you dampen a few joints; just try to keep them clean and dry for the grout. After the application is complete, let the sealer dry completely (follow the manufacturer's recommendations) before you begin grout-ing. Stone tiles, which are not fired with a protective glaze, should be sealed a second time for protection *after* you have grouted.

Sealing grout

After your tile is grouted and dry, it's time to apply a grout sealer. As with tile sealers, we prefer water-based products because they're safer to use and less odorous. One of the easiest ways to apply sealer to grout joints is with a commercially available plastic applicator bottle that has a brush or roller tip.

Simply fill the bottle and adjust the twist top so that the right amount flows onto the joint. As it flows out, the sealer is absorbed by the grout and disappears, evidenced by the temporary darkening of the grout color ❶. If the sealer puddles on the grout, reduce the flow slightly by adjusting the applicator tip. Use the applicator tip to move the excess sealer onto dry joints or use a cloth to mop it up. If a small amount of sealer flows onto the tile, just wipe it up with a clean cloth or paper towel. ❷.

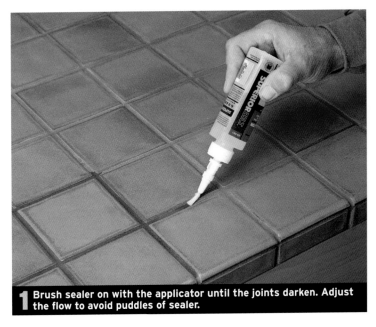

1 Brush sealer on with the applicator until the joints darken. Adjust the flow to avoid puddles of sealer.

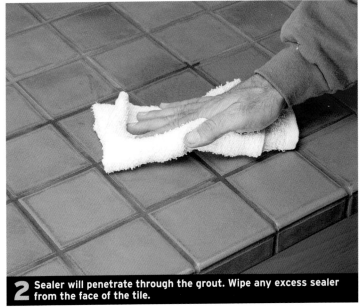

2 Sealer will penetrate through the grout. Wipe any excess sealer from the face of the tile.

SEALING TERRA-COTTA PAVERS

1 Most Saltillo finishing systems consist of two or three products.

2 Wipe the sealer on evenly, coating the tile face and grout joints with a damp paintbrush.

4 Roll the sealer onto the floor, making sure tile faces and grout joints are fully covered.

or

5 You may use a pad-type applicator in lieu of a brush or roller to apply floor-finishing products.

Terra-cotta pavers look great when treated with a top finish. Applied in addition to a sealer, a top finish enhances durability, ease of cleaning, and gives the tiles a great, sophisticated look. There are myriad finishing systems made for sealing pavers and Saltillos, each offering a slightly different look and finish.

→ See "Sealers," p. 87.

As always, we prefer to use water-based finishes because they have a lower toxicity, have less odor, and are easier to clean up than solvent-based products. Just make sure that the finish you select is compatible with the tile sealer you used by checking

with the manufacturer; the wrong product can ruin the look of an entire job.

Most terra-cotta finishing systems consist of two or three products **1**. The first is a sealer that's applied to the tile before grouting.

In addition to preventing the grout from staining the tile, this sealer makes it easier to clean the grout from the tile faces during wipe down. The second product is a topcoat finish that, depending on the particular product, gives the tile either a natural, matte, or glossy finish. The top coat is usually applied in several applications. Some finishing systems include a third product: a wax-type finish that is easy to reapply to make tile look fresh again, after long usage

has dulled the finish. Some manufacturers will combine the second and third steps in a single product, for ease of use.

The application of any terra-cotta finishing product is quite straightforward. If you're finishing a small area, use a plastic bucket and a brush, sponge, or clean rag as an applicator. Brush the sealer on evenly, beginning with the perimeter of a manageable area, probably about 4 sq. ft., coating the tile face and grout joints **2**. Let it dry according to the directions and apply a second or third coat as necessary. For larger floors, apply the sealer with a paint roller with a 1/4-in. nap mounted on a pole handle (this will save your back). Pour the liquid into

SEALING NATURAL STONE

3 For large floors, apply the sealer with a paint roller with a ¼-in. nap, mounted on a pole handle.

6 Apply subsequent coats of floor-finishing products at right angles to previous coats.

Natural stone does not have a glazed surface and is so porous that it must be sealed before grouting to prevent the grout from staining the stone (the exception is if you wish to fill the porous stone's cavities).

→ **See "Natural Stone," p. 230.**

Sealing stone also prevents the grout from filling every pore of the tile's surface, saving you hours of grief from having to scrub down the tiles after grouting.

You can use the same sealer that you'd use to seal other porous tiles or products specially made for stone. For best results, you should seal natural stone tiles twice: The first coat, applied before grouting, provides protection from grout staining; the second coat, applied after grouting adds protection to both the grout and the tile. Apply both coats with a sponge, following the manufacturer's directions on the particular sealer product you use.

Many stone tiles show their colors more intensely after being treated with a product called an enhancer. You can get an idea of what stone treated this way will look like by sponging a tile with water. Enhancer is applied after the installation is sealed and cured, usually after about 1 week. If you decide to use an enhancer, make sure to use a sealer made by the same manufacturer and follow their application instructions to the letter.

a 5-gal. pail fitted with a bucket grid ❸, dip the roller into the bucket and roll it a few times across the grid, to remove excess liquid. This prevents the sealer from going on too thick. Roll the sealer onto the floor, making sure the tile faces and grout joints are fully covered ❹. If some puddling occurs, use the roller to spread the finish to adjacent areas. You may also use a pad-type applicator instead of a roller ❺. Let the sealer dry according to the directions, then apply the second and (if used) third finishing products, brushing or rolling each on in a perpendicular direction to the previous coat ❻.

A penetrating sealer applied to the surface of stone will prevent grout staining. Tiles will temporarily appear darker.

ROUTINE MAINTENANCE

There are many versatile cleaning products **to help you maintain the beauty of your tile and grout.**

The Hoover® React™ vacuums **are designed for use on various floor types—from tile to wood or carpet—as they adjust to each type by "reacting" automatically.**

The easiest way to keep tile clean and looking like new is regular, light cleaning to keep dust and grime from building up—especially in the grout. Cleaning methods vary a little, depending on whether the surface you're maintaining is a floor, counter, or tub enclosure.

Floors

To keep dust at bay on a tile floor, you can sweep with a broom, but an electric broom or hard-flour vacuum cleaner will be more effective. When you need to scrub grime from a tile floor, always use a mild cleaner that does not contain dyes or bleach. We encourage you to stay away from the traditional mopping methods, as they tend to dissolve the dirt into a solution that ends up in the grout joints. For large and small floors, electric devices such as hard-floor vacuums, with or without steam or mopping capabilities, will be your first line of defense to keep your tile and grout like new.

Counters and backsplashes

To keep your tiled counters in a kitchen or bathroom free of dirt, crumbs, and other small debris, vacuum them occasionally with a small portable vacuum, such as a Dustbuster®. For heavier cleaning of counters and tiled walls in a bathroom or tub enclosure, use a damp nonabrasive foam sponge to wipe surfaces down with water or, when necessary, a mild clear or white dish detergent free from dyes.

TRADE SECRET
Consumer magazines often give low ratings to the "miracle" automatic shower cleaning products you see on television. You'll get better results with regular cleaning and by wiping down the shower walls after every use.

Incidentally, a great way to keep kitchen surfaces clean is to do your food prep tasks atop a cutting board instead of on top of the tile itself. Putting a clear acrylic board or plastic kitchen mat over a high-maintenance area near a refrigerator or stove or under a coffeemaker not only helps contain spills but cuts down on wear and tear to the tile.

Showers and tub surrounds

Cleaning and maintaining bathrooms require much of the same routine care as mentioned for other areas of the home. You can use the same products and methods for routine cleaning of the floor, counter, and wall areas. However, since tub and shower areas can hold lots of moisture, they need daily attention or mildew will proliferate and hard water deposits can build up.

The simplest way to keep these areas clean is to either squeegee the walls or wipe them down with a towel after you shower or bathe. By removing excess moisture, mildew will have trouble getting a toehold in your bathroom and lime scale and other mineral deposits won't build up on your shower or tub enclosure tile.

To remove grout stains **or pot marks, sprinkle some Bon Ami® on a damp surface and scrub with a foam sponge.**

A cutting board or mat **will save wear and tear on your countertop and catch errant drops or spills.**

Using a squeegee or towel **to wipe down your tiled walls after showering helps prevent mildew.**

Dealing with mildew Mildew is a type of mold, most often seen as black dots or streaks that form on tile or grout in damp, warm areas. Mildew needs three things to make it thrive: Moisture, something it can feed on, and a warm environment. Around your kitchen and bathroom sinks—and especially your shower and tub—these items are plentiful. But if you remove one of the three, mildew cannot grow. While it's the most labor intensive, cleaning and drying your tile regularly is your best defense against mildew. An easier way to prevent mildew from forming is to keep tiled areas well ventilated, via an open window or fan. If you have a bathroom fan, turn it on every time you bathe (some fans have a timer that can be set to shut off after 30 minutes). If ventilation is a problem, wipe down your tile after every use with a dry cloth.

GROUT

1 Most tiles will retain their luster, but the grout can attract stains or become dingy over time.

2 For stain removal, dampen the surface and sprinkle cleanser directly on the grout joints.

3 Rub the moist cleanser paste into the grout joints and let it do its work for about 5 minutes.

4 Scrub the grout and tile surface with the rough, nonmetallic side of the sponge.

WHAT CAN GO WRONG

Stay away from tile cleaning products that contain bleach and/or acids. Bleach will appear to clean your grout but that's because it is actually removing the first layer of the material. Over time, you will have less and less grout, until you find you need to regrout the entire job.

Most tiles clean up very well and continue to look good even decades after installation. Unfortunately, grout joints tend to collect dirt and stains and will quickly look grungy if not cleaned regularly **1**. If you find a stain in the grout, try removing it with a scouring powder such as Bon Ami. Apply the powder with a nonmetallic scrubbing pad and rub the area gently **2**. If at first you don't succeed, cover the stain with a thick layer of wet powder, let it penetrate for 5 minutes to 10 minutes, scrub, then rinse thoroughly. Do not use colored cleansers, such as Ajax® and Comet®, as they can actually discolor or damage the grout over time.

If the grout has been neglected for a long time and is heavily stained, try covering it with a mixture of scouring powder and hot tap water. Rub the powder into the grout joints with a gloved fingertip, then let it sit for 10 minutes to 15 minutes **3**. Scrub the area with a firm-bristle scrub brush or nonmetallic scrubbing pad **4**. If this technique doesn't produce success, you can use a stronger cleaner like sulfamic acid, phosphoric acid, or a liquid cleaner like Bright Glaze®, but only occasionally; regular usage will eat away your grout. If the grout simply will not come clean, one alternative is to paint it with a grout recolorant.

➡ See "Grout Recolorant," p. 86.

NATURAL STONE AND TERRA-COTTA

For the most part, natural stone and terra-cotta tiles can be swept, vacuumed, and otherwise maintained like other tiles. However, these materials are porous, and even properly sealed tiles can absorb stains that aren't wiped up quickly ❶. Fortunately, you can remove small stains fairly easily with specialty stone-specific cleaners (available at tile stores and home improvement centers) that are formulated for cleaning natural stone and terra-cotta without etching or damaging the tiles.

To remove a stain, you apply a poultice of the cleaning product over the stain. Apply the cleaner straight from the container, spread it over the stain ❷, then cover the area with plastic wrap or aluminum foil and tape the edges ❸. Leave this area alone for 24 hours. Remove the covering and wipe the tile clean ❹. In most cases, the drying poultice will remove the stain ❺. If this doesn't work, contact a professional stone cleaner or restorer (look in your phone book or check online for a marble cleaning service).

Cleaning glass tile

You'll be happy to know that cleaning glass tile is as simple as cleaning your windows. A spray-on glass cleaning solution keeps all your glass tile surfaces shiny and clear. Just be sure to stay away from using a colored cleaner (such as blue Windex®) as it may stain or color the grout. And do not use any product containing abrasives or acids because they could scratch or etch the glass. It's best to spray a soft cloth or cleaning mitt with the cleaner and then wipe down the surface rather than spraying the solution directly onto the tile.

1 Stains in stone or porous tiles require a bit more work to remove.

2 Spread a thick layer of poultice on the stain.

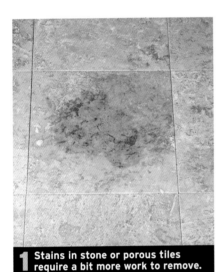

3 Cover the poultice with aluminum foil or plastic wrap for 24 hours.

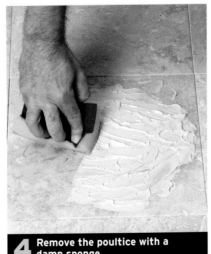

4 Remove the poultice with a damp sponge.

5 Using a poultice can return your stone floor back to its original beauty. Be sure and reapply sealer.

ASSESSING TILE REPAIRS

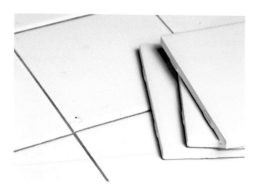

If one of your tiles **ever becomes chipped,** you'll be glad that you've saved some replacement tiles.

A decorative tile of the same size can sometimes be substituted for a chipped one if you can't get replacement tiles.

Computer-matched enamel paint **can make cracks in irreplaceable tiles much less noticeable.**

Tools for any tile repair: **trusty hammer, carbide-tipped chisel, and sharp utility knife.**

Even though tile is a durable material, tiled surfaces can become chipped or damaged. Before you rush into any tile repair, there are some considerations. First, you want to be sure that you have enough replacement tile for the repair, including a few extras, in case you accidently damage surrounding tiles during removal. If you haven't saved extra tiles from the original installation, you may not be able to replace them with tiles from the same dye lot, so the color may not match exactly. If you purchase new tiles, make sure that they are exact replacements by checking them against the installed tiles. Sometimes you can use your creativity and replace damaged tiles with decorative tiles of the same size.

You'll also need grout that matches the grout originally used in the installation, if it is still available. If your grout color isn't available, look for the closest color match (the lack of matching grout may change your decision to replace tiles).

Removing damaged tile

Despite the common misconception, it's not at all easy to pop out a damaged tile for replacement. Be sure you've considered the risks we've just mentioned before you attempt even a simple repair. If you're ready to tackle this repair, the safest way to remove damaged tile is with a good old-fashioned hammer and a carbide-tipped chisel.

It's tedious work that you wouldn't want for your day job, but it gets the job done with the least possibility of collateral damage to surrounding tiles. For tiles bigger than 8 in. sq., we sometimes employ a grinder to save some time (and impact damage to our wrists and hands), but the hammer and chisel are still needed to complete the removal.

Repairs not to attempt

Some tile repairs just aren't worth the time and trouble they would take. Depending on the nature and location of the damage, a tile repair might actually exacerbate an underlying problem, such as a weak substrate or poorly bonded tile, or even create a new problem by cracking or chipping tiles adjacent to the one you wish to replace.

Two common places to encounter damaged tiles are high-use areas, such as above the dishwasher and near the kitchen sink. If the installed tiles in these areas aren't extremely durable, they can quickly become damaged. Unfortunately, such locations are usually poorly supported—there's no cabinet frame and the repeated pounding required when chiseling out a damaged tile can easily damage a larger area and lead to a more extensive repair, possibly the replacement of the entire countertop. We rarely recommend that tiles in these areas be replaced. Touch them up with enamel paint, or leave the repair to a professional tile installer.

REMOVING GROUT

A A utility knife can remove softer grout. Use both hands to steady the knife.

B Remove down to the setting bed with the knife.

efore tile removal begins, you need to remove the grout surrounding the tile **A**. This greatly lowers the risk of chipping the glaze on adjacent tiles. The grout found in old tile jobs laid on a mortar bed is often too hard to remove, in which case you can proceed with the hammer and chisel removal.

➔ See "Removing Tile with a Hammer and Chisel," p. 250.

Softer grout can be removed either with a razor knife, a grout saw, or with a portable electric tool. A razor knife fitted with a sharp blade works great on grout, especially if the joints are no wider than 1/8 in. Simply work the tip of the knife carefully into the grout and slice along both sides of the joint, cutting and removing the grout a little at a time all the way around the damaged tile **B**.

A grout saw can be used for removing grout in joints that are 1/8 in. or wider. Hold the grip of the saw firmly in your hand and use a back and forth motion to remove the old grout. Hold the saw steady so you won't risk nicking or chipping the adjacent tiles **C**. This is the slow way to go but dust is minimal. For faster grout removal on more extensive repairs, you can fit a standard reciprocating saw with a special grout-cutting blade **D**.

C A hand-held carbide grout saw can be used to remove grout around a cracked or chipped tile.

D A carbide grout blade attached to your reciprocating saw quickly removes grout from around tiles.

To replace a tile grouted with epoxy grout, you'll first need to soften the grout with a heat gun. It can then be scraped out with a utility knife.

REMOVING TILE WITH A HAMMER AND CHISEL

1 Use a hammer and chisel to nick the top part of the glaze to create a divot.

2 Drill holes in the surface of the tile to give the chisel some starting points.

3 Use the chisel to remove small fragments of tile.

4 Hammer and chisel out the remaining parts of the tile with great care.

5 Use a razor knife to remove any remaining grout with caution. The cleaner the area, the easier it will be to fit the new tile.

Once the grout is removed around the tile you're replacing, place some towels or tarps around the work area, as tile chips can fly far.

First, use the corner of a carbide-tipped chisel to create a series of small dimples **1**, which will keep the drill bit from skipping across the tile. Use a masonry bit in an electric drill to bore a series of holes in the center and along the edges of the damaged tile, staying about 1/2 in. away from the grout joints **2**. The holes will help the tile break out in small pieces and protect adjacent tiles from cracking. Using a hammer and carbide-tipped chisel, break the tile into small pieces, working carefully from the center to the outside of the tile **3**. Hammer as gently as you can; pounding may cause cracks in the tile's substrate (backerboard, mortar bed) to travel, damaging additional tiles. Do not worry about cleaning off the substrate at this time. As you near the edge, chisel the remaining tile carefully and break it away from the grout joints **4**. *Do not* hammer in the grout joints themselves, or you're likely to chip adjacent tiles. After all the tile pieces have been removed, carefully carve off any remaining grout with a razor knife **5**.

WARNING

Wear safety glasses when breaking tile with a hammer and chisel. Chips can fly, causing permanent eye damage if you get hit.

REMOVING TILE WITH A GRINDER

If you are comfortable using an angle grinder and you don't mind the mess, you can remove tiles more quickly by first grinding slots in the tiles, then using a hammer and chisel to knock the pieces free. This method works best with bigger, more durable tiles (porcelain, granite) with larger grout joints, as it's more difficult to control the grinder on smaller tiles.

Start by sealing doorways and covering adjacent areas and furniture with plastic sheeting as necessary.

Using a special tile-and-stone cutting blade mounted in the grinder, cut along the inside of the damaged tile, about ½ in. in from the edges. Next, cut an X in the center of the tile, extending the legs almost all the way to the corners ❶. Be sure to hold the grinder carefully as the tool's torque can take you by surprise. Cut slowly to avoid binding and skittering into the next tile. To reduce the grinding mess, you or a friend may hold the end of a vacuum hose right behind the grinding wheel to suck up the dust while cutting ❷. Now use a carbide-tipped chisel and a hammer to break the tile up, starting at the center and working outward (see the facing page). The edges will fall away from the grout joints as you work. As mentioned before, never chisel near adjacent tiles, as you'll likely chip or break them.

1 Use an angle grinder to cut an X before removing the rest of the tile.

2 A vacuum held near the grinder will reduce the amount of airborne dust.

WARNING

Grinding generates lots of fine dust. Protect yourself by wearing safety glasses, ear protection, gloves, respirator, and work clothes.

The tap test Large areas of missing or cracked grout in older tile installations often indicate that the tile is no longer properly bonded to the substrate, possibly due to poor workmanship or other problems. The easiest way to detect a tile-bonding problem is to perform the tap test. Take a coin or key and tap on and around the offending tile. The sound difference will be obvious: Well-bonded tiles produce a very solid sound. A hollow sound usually indicates either missing thinset or a loose tile.

If you detect a small hollow area, perhaps around just the corner of a tile, and everything else seems solid, it usually means that the tile needed a bit more thinset when it was installed. If the tile isn't cracked, leave it alone. If the tile seems solid but grout is loose, remove the loose grout and regrout the area, as described on p. 260.

If only one or two tiles sound hollow and the rest are solid, remove and replace just the bad tiles. Large hollow-sounding areas usually indicate a more serious job failure caused by either an improper substrate, too much movement in the substrate, or improper use of tile-bonding adhesive. This is a much greater problem that may be resolved only by complete removal of the tile work and installation of new tiles. If you're in doubt, it's best to contact a tile professional to evaluate the situation.

SETTING REPLACEMENT TILE

1 Use a chisel to remove small chunks of thinset but be careful when you do. It is *very* easy to chip another tile.

2 Sponge any remaining grit or dust from the area to be reset, dampening the substrate at the same time.

3 Dry-fit the replacement tile into its new place of honor on the countertop.

4 Apply thinset to the back of your replacement tile, especially the corners.

Once your old, damaged tile has been removed, you must remove the layer of thinset or other tile-adhesive material under it, so that the new tile will fit flush with the remaining tiles in the repair area **1**. Use a carbide-tipped chisel to carefully remove all the adhesive material until the substrate is clean. If your tile is set on a concrete or mortar bed, a wallpaper scraper with a 4-in. blade is very handy for scraping the adhesive off (if room allows). If your substrate is a soft

material, like drywall or plaster, scrape or chisel *very* carefully so you won't damage it. Too much damage, and you'll need to replace the backing, which is a real hassle.

Once the substrate is clean, vacuum or sponge down the entire repair area to remove any remaining dust and debris **2**. Now dry-fit your new tile: It should sit slightly below the surrounding tiles to leave room for thinset **3**. If the replacement tile sits too high, remove any grout or thinset that is

5 Fit the tile into place and use your fingers to check that it is flush with adjacent tiles.

6 Work the grout into the joints with your finger.

interfering. Mix up a little thinset (whichever kind is appropriate for your type of tile).

➡ See "Choosing an Adhesive," pp. 77-80.

Back-butter the tile **4** and slip it place, pressing it in with your fingers **5**. On vertical surfaces, use wedges or spacers to hold the tile in place until dry. Grout around the new tile **6**, and you're done.

TOUCHING UP TILES

Sometimes removing and replacing damaged tiles is too risky a job, especially if the tile is unusual and replacement tiles simply aren't available. One way to make chipped or cracked tiles look a little better is to touch them up with a little paint. If you have an old tile, take it to the paint store for comparison and/or color matching and purchase a small can of enamel paint **1**. Use a small brush to dab the paint onto the damaged areas of the tile and wipe off any excess paint with a bit of paper towel **2**. You can perform somewhat less durable touch ups with nail polish and even typing correction fluid.

1 Find the right color. Computer-matched enamel paint can make cracks much less noticeable.

2 Rub some paint into the crack and wipe off any excess. Keep the paint off of the grout joints.

TILE REPAIR AFTER PLUMBING VALVE CHANGE

After many years, it is not uncommon to find out that your shower or tub valve has a leak, causing you to hire a plumber who will tear apart your lovely tiled wall to replace the valve. While most plumbers will remove the tile to do the valve change, very few will repair the actual tile work. This section will show you how to complete the repair and maintain any waterproofing.

Replacement tiles

If you are fortunate enough to have tile remaining from the original installation, those tiles will be your replacement tiles, which makes your repair easy. If you don't have the original tiles (or don't have enough for the repair), you'll need to find replacement tiles. If you contracted or did the work yourself, contact the store that supplied your tile to see if they have any remaining stock. If you don't know the origin of the tile, check with a reputable store in your area.

Take a photo of your tile, and/or, if your plumber has removed the tile, take any piece or broken chunk of the tile to the store with you. If the tile is no longer available, you'll have to use a different size or color of tile to repair the area. If this is the case, you might want to use a decorative tile or create a border to change the size or orientation of the replacement tiles. You could also choose a tile in a contrasting color to look more intentional, rather than have your repair look like a patch (as shown in the repair-over-mud example here).

After the tile is removed and the valve is replaced, you'll be able to see whether your tile was installed over a mud bed or over backerboard. The following two sections will show you how to repair either situation. We will also deal with methods to maintain your waterproofing.

A plumber has **replaced the old valves, and the wall is ready for repair.**

TRADE SECRET

Assess your installation to see if there is waterproof paper around the valve repair. If you find that there's paper, take care to leave it as intact as possible.

Repair over mud bed

You need to protect the surrounding area before you begin to work **❶**. Tape off the top of the tub and cover the bottom with a blanket or drop cloth and/or work surface to protect the tub or shower floor from dirt, dust, water, and damage from a dropped tool **❷**. Protect the new valve stems with tape or cardboard sleeves.

❶ Always protect the bottom and top of the tub before commencing work.

❷ For the repair, a work surface will be helpful for protection.

3 Drill through the old thinset and tile to get to the old mortar bed with as little impact on surrounding areas as possible.

4 A vacuum will keep the dust at a minimum, but you may need an extra pair of hands to assist you.

5 Use a hammer and chisel with care to remove the remaining tiles and mortar bed for the repair.

6 Cut any wire or lath but leave 1½ in. to lap over your new wire reinforcing for your mortar bed.

7 Overlap the existing waterproof paper with new waterproof paper, from bottom to top.

8 Fit and screw your backerboard into place.

If there are additional chipped tiles to be removed, take care of those tiles first (being careful not to drill into any plumbing pipes) **3**, **4**, **5**. Now, clip away any reinforcing wire, leaving about 1½ in. around the perimeter for overlapping purposes **6**. Once the area is clear, tuck waterproof paper under the paper at the top and over any paper at the bottom of the opening **7**. Cut and install a piece of backerboard for backing **8**. Cut a piece of reinforcing wire or metal lath to size and attach to the backerboard **9**. Wrap the cut perimeter wires over the board **10**.

>> >> >>

9 Cut and fit reinforcing wire to lay over the backerboard.

10 Bend the old reinforcing wire over the new lath or wire.

TILE REPAIR AFTER PLUMBING VALVE CHANGE (CONTINUED)

11 Apply mortar until the wire is completely covered.

12 Use a scrap piece of board or other material to smooth out the mortar.

13 For further protection, apply a waterproof membrane with a brush.

14 After the membrane has cured, lay tiles and use a level to ensure that they are even with existing areas.

15 Set replacement tiles as shown on p. 252. To drill holes for the valves, refer to p. 64.

16 The repair is grouted and finished.

Mix a small amount of brick mortar mix and spread it over the entire area **11**. Use a scrap piece of wood or backerboard to smooth the mud slightly below the existing mud bed **12**. Hold a tile on the mortar near the existing wall tiles to check that you will have room for your new tile adhered with some thinset behind it. Let cure overnight.

The following day, brush a generous coating of antifracture/waterproofing membrane (p. 72) over the entire area of the repair **13**. Allow to dry according to the manufacturer's instructions.

Set your replacement tiles flush with the existing installation using modified thinset **14**, grout, and allow appropriate curing time before you or your plumber set the finish plumbing **15**, **16**.

1 Tape and protect the new valve and the surrounding work area.

2 Scrape the old thinset off the backerboard with the flat edge of your margin trowel.

3 Mark out plumb and level lines around the damaged area that will be replaced.

Repair over backerboard

If you're making a repair over tile set on backerboard, protect the area and remove any chipped tiles as you did for the repair over mud **1**. Scrape or chip off residual thinset from the existing backerboard **2**. With a small level, mark out a rectangle or square on the backerboard just beyond the damaged area **3**. Cut to these lines by scoring, then cutting with a utility knife, and remove any additional board with tile nippers **4**, **5**.

>> >> >>

4 Use a utility knife to score along the marked lines.

5 Tile nippers come in handy in these awkward places to remove the backerboard up to your lines.

TILE REPAIR AFTER PLUMBING VALVE CHANGE (CONTINUED)

6 Drill screws through the existing backerboard to mount a support piece of wood.

7 Cut the replacement piece of backerboard and set it in place.

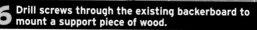

8 Screw the board into the support piece (left) and an available stud (right).

Screw in blocking to reinforce and bolster the repair piece **6**. Cut the repair piece to size, slightly smaller than the opening you just created, and screw it in place **7**, **8**.

9 Force caulk into the gaps, smooth even with the surface, and allow to dry.

10 Place fiberglass mesh over the seams to increase the strength of the repair.

Caulk generously around the perimeter of the patch, then flatten and allow drying time **9**. Add fiberglass mesh at the seams to reinforce the repair and coat with antifracture/waterproofing membrane (see p. 72) **10**, **11**. Set the replacement tiles with modified thinset, checking that they lay as flat as possible to the existing installation. Grout and allow to cure before setting your finish plumbing.

11 The repair is now ready for waterproofing, setting tile, and grouting.

REPAIRING GROUT

1 Small areas of missing grout can easily be repaired.

2 Check for any loose grout and lift it out carefully.

3 Use a knife to clean out debris in open joints.

4 Pull and peel away any old caulk that comes out with ease.

5 Spread the grout into the joint with a gloved or naked finger.

6 Wipe the grout with a sponge, blending the new grout with the old.

Grout that's cracked, heavily discolored, or missing in small areas is unsightly, even if the surrounding tile is in perfect shape. It's tempting to touch up these areas by simply adding a little new grout over the problem. But to perform a longer-lasting repair, you should remove as much of the old grout as possible in the affected areas. This is because new grout doesn't stick well to old grout; it needs to adhere to the substrate that supports both the tile and the grout.

To repair small grout problems on a tiled area, such as this bathroom sink ❶, start by lifting any of the old grout using a fresh blade in a utility knife ❷. Remove only what comes out easily, as digging too hard might chip adjacent tiles. In joints where most of the grout is already missing, use a utility knife to carefully clean dirt and debris from the gap ❸. Cut away any old caulk you find around the sink ❹ and sweep the area clean to remove any remaining debris. Mix a small amount of new grout and let it slake.

➡ **See "Mixing Grout," p. 218.**

Push the grout into the cleaned-out joints with your fingers ❺. Allow the grout to set up for 5 minutes or 10 minutes, then shape and wipe the repaired areas with a sponge, working carefully to blend the new grout in with the old wherever they meet ❻. Let the newly grouted areas dry, then do the final polishing and cleaning on those areas. Now you're ready to apply a new bead of caulk around the sink. In many cases, it's better to apply new caulk over old grout than to take the risk of digging it out. After applying the caulk ❼, smooth the bead with your finger ❽. Although the new grout and caulk may not match exactly, you'll end up with a tiled surface that's free of cracks and gaps ❾.

7 Caulk any areas that typically experience movement, as between sink and tile.

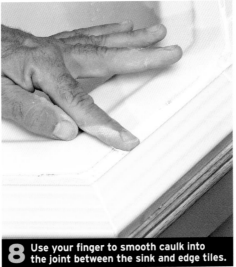

8 Use your finger to smooth caulk into the joint between the sink and edge tiles.

9 New grout and caulk refresh a classic countertop.

REPLACING OLD GROUT WITH CAULK

It's not uncommon to find missing or cracked grout in areas like the junction between sink and tile, counters and backsplashes, edges between tiled walls, and where a tiled surface meets another material (a wood floor) ❶. Grout problems in these areas are due to naturally occurring movement between surfaces, which will always cause the grout to crack. You can repair these areas by simply replacing the grout with flexible caulk. Carefully remove as much of the damaged grout as possible.

➡ See "Removing Grout," p. 249.

Clean out the joint, then run a bead of caulk ❷. This will stay flexible and eliminate any future cracking.

1 A tile splash should always be caulked at the wood and tile juncture.

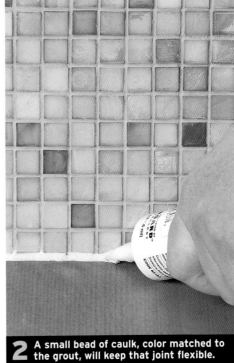

2 A small bead of caulk, color matched to the grout, will keep that joint flexible.

DEALING WITH EFFLORESCENCE

Efflorescence is a fancy word for a white haze that sometimes forms on grout and tile. Efflorescence is due to excessive moisture that leaches salts from the grout (or the mortar or concrete substrate) and deposits it on the surface. Although efflorescence can affect many different kinds of tile, you'll see it most often on low-fired terra-cotta and Saltillo tiles because of their porous nature. The haze may occur on the grout joints only, or it may show up on the surface of the tile itself.

You can often remove efflorescence haze from small areas by washing it off with a 50/50 solution of white vinegar and water. For large areas, use a haze remover or sulfamic acid mixture ❶. If this is a new tile installation, you must wait 7 days to 10 days before acid washing. You will need rubber gloves, safety glasses, old work clothes (unless acid-washed jeans is your style), a non-metallic bucket for the acid, a 5-gal. plastic wash-down bucket, a nylon-bristle scrub brush or toothbrush, and several new sponges. If you're using sulfamic acid, mix 2 oz. to 3 oz. of the powder with 1 gal. of water. Saturate the affected area with clean water an hour before acid washing ❷, so the moisture has time to penetrate through the grout joints. Before you apply the acid solution, rewet small areas at a time to prevent acid burn of the grout joints and tile. Apply the acid to the wet surface and agitate with the brush ❸. Work on a small, 2-sq.-ft. to 3-sq.-ft., area at a time. Wipe down the tile with a wet, clean sponge and then wash the surface with fresh water several times to remove all the acid from the tile and grout.

1 Sulfamic acid dissolves the efflorescence that clouds the beauty of your original grout color.

2 Always wet the joints with water an hour before applying the sulfamic acid solution.

3 Use gloves and goggles when you acid wash the area. A small brush helps you agitate the solution into the joints.

RESEALING GROUT

If you've sealed your grout with a penetrating sealer, it can last up to 20 years, depending on usage. In a kitchen or other high-use area, you might need a stronger defense against stains and dirt. For this purpose, there are products on the market that reseal as you clean. These are great time-savers and provide additional protection.

You can easily check the integrity of the sealer on any job by putting a few drops of water on the grout ❶. If it beads up right away, your grout is still adequately sealed. If the water is absorbed quickly, it's time to reseal the grout. Before you reapply sealer to the old grout, you'll want to clean the entire area thoroughly and let it dry ❷. Apply the sealer just as you would to a new tile installation ❸.

1 Drops of water will bead up on the grout if it's still sealed.

2 Clean area thoroughly before resealing.

3 Reapply sealer.

TRADE SECRET

To protect a floor tile, put doormats at the inside and outside of every entrance to the house. This reduces much of the dirt, sand, and grit that clings to shoes and can wear down the tile's glaze and sealer, along with creating additional housekeeping work for you.

RESEALING NATURAL STONE AND TERRA-COTTA

Sealers used on natural stone and terra-cotta wear off due to normal usage, cleaning, and foot traffic. You can check the effectiveness of tile sealers by dripping water on the face of the tile. If it beads up, the sealer is still good, but if it is absorbed, you'll need to reseal the tile. Use a penetrating sealer for a natural look or a top finish sealer for a glossy appearance.

After thoroughly cleaning the surface of the tile, check the compatibility of the new sealer with any old sealer remaining on the tile. Brush a small amount of sealer on a tile in an inconspicuous location. If the new sealer is absorbed, seal the rest of the surface.

➜ See "Sealing Terra-Cotta Pavers," p. 240 and "Sealing Natural Stone," p. 241.

If the sealer beads up, you need to strip the old finish off the tile before resealing it. Unfortunately, stripping tile requires the use of toxic products and a good knowledge of chemicals and techniques. Our recommendation is that you leave this to a floor-care professional.

Resealing your stone or tile **takes a minimum amount of effort and gives maximum results in maintaining the surface.**

GLOSSARY

ACRYLIC (ADDITIVE) A liquid additive that greatly increases the strength and flexibility of thinset and grout. Many thinsets and grouts have this incorporated into their formula and all you do is add water.

BACK-BUTTER The process of spreading thinset adhesive on the back of a tile with a margin trowel or a notched trowel to set a tile or supplement thinset on a tile that sits too low. The entire tile must be evenly covered.

BACKERBOARD Cement-based sheet material that can be used as a substrate on floors, counters, and backsplashes.

BACKSPLASH The vertical wall surface above a countertop.

BUTT JOINT A tight joint made by setting two tiles so they touch one another without spacers between them.

BEATER OR BEATING BLOCK A commercially available flat block of wood that has a rubber coating on one side to protect tile surfaces. The block is held in your hand and the wood face of the block is hit with a hammer. This action "beats" the tile into the thinset.

BISQUE The clay body of a glazed tile.

BRICK OR SUBWAY PATTERN A design created by setting a row of tile so it is offset by half its width relative to the previous row of tile.

CARBIDE-TIPPED CHISEL A chisel with a hard carbide edge. It is very durable and, when used in conjunction with a hammer, excellent for tile repairs.

CAULK A flexible material used between tile and other materials to allow for movement.

CERAMIC TILE Clay that has been glazed on one side and fired.

DECK The horizontal surface of a countertop.

DECORATIVE AND/OR RELIEF TILE A painted, textured, or patterned tile that is distinct from the field tiles.

DOWN ANGLE A field tile with two adjacent rounded-over glazed edges. Used to finish outside corners of bullnose trim.

EFFLORESCENCE Whitish deposit from salts that can surface on porous tile and grout. This can happen to any cement-based product and can be removed with the proper treatment.

EPOXY (THINSET ADHESIVE) A two-part, expensive adhesive used for very specialized applications. Not necessary for most tile installations.

EXPANSION JOINT A joint in the layout that will be filled with flexible caulk, allowing for movement. Usually located against adjacent walls, countertops, and unlike surfaces.

EXTRUDED TILE Bisque that is pressed through a die to create a shape before firing.

FIELD TILE A full-size tile in the main area of the installation.

GLAZE Not the stuff on doughnuts. A hard surface fired onto one side of a tile that usually makes a glossy surface.

GRANITE A very hard stone that comes in a range of colors and must be sealed.

GROUT, SANDED AND NONSANDED The cement-based mix used between tiles to fill the joints. Nonsanded is used for joints $1/8$ in. or less. Sanded is used for joints larger than $1/8$ in.

HARDIBOARD Cement-based backerboard manufactured by the James Hardie® Company that is easy to cut and nail. It is available in ¼-in. and ½-in. thicknesses.

LEDGER BOARD A straight piece of wood used as a place marker and starting point to set wall tile.

LEVEL Flat or horizontally straight.

LINER A thin or narrow tile used as a decorative piece. Often used to delineate or outline a pattern.

LISTELLO A border tile that usually has a relief or raised pattern.

MASTIC Mixed, ready-to-set water-based setting adhesive that has less bonding strength than a modified thinset.

MODIFIED THINSET Thinset powder that contains acrylic additive in a dry form.

MOSAIC Any tile that is 2 in. or less, in any shape or material.

MUD WORK The oldest method for creating a substrate and the best for maintaining plumb and level work surfaces for tile. Requires professional skill to mix and place the sand, cement, and lime mixture.

PLUMB Any vertical surface that is at a perfect right angle to the horizon.

PORCELAIN TILE High-fired, very dense tile that is excellent for floors and other high-use areas.

QUARTER-ROUND Rounded tiles that complete 90° angles at wall edges and between horizontal and vertical tiled surfaces. Traditionally used for covering the edge of a mud installation.

RADIUS TRIM A tile piece with a rounded edge so that it can negotiate its way around a thick substrate.

RUBBER FLOAT A rubber or other soft-sided trowel used for spreading grout.

RUBBING OR CARBORUNDUM STONE A handheld stone used for smoothing cut edges of tile or softening edges of cut natural stone tiles.

SEALER Protective coating for grout or tile. It can be penetrating or surface finish.

SLAKE A time-out or rest period between mixing thinset or grout with liquid and using it, allowing the liquid to penetrate and dissolve the ingredients for a homogeneous mix.

SLATE Stone composed of shale and clay.

SLIP SHEET One type of antifracture membrane that comes in sheet form.

SNAP CUTTER OR CUTTING BOARD A manually operated flat board with a scoring wheel used for scoring and snapping tile for cuts.

SPACER Plastic or rubber pieces in different shapes and sizes that keep tiles equally spaced.

SUBFLOOR The wood surface found underneath flooring attached to the floor joists. Usually plywood in newer homes or 1x6 solid lumber in older homes.

SUBSTRATE Any surface, whether a manufactured one like concrete backerboard or an existing surface such as concrete to which tile is affixed.

SURFACE BULLNOSE TRIM A field tile with one rounded-over glazed and fired edge.

TERRA-COTTA OR PAVER TILES Clay tiles fired at low temperatures. Their surfaces must be sealed.

THINSET A powder that is mixed with water or acrylic to compose a strong bonding adhesive for setting tile.

TRIM TILE Specialty tiles that work as finish ends for tile work. Trim tiles will finish the field tiles and come in different profiles such as surface bullnose and quarter-rounds.

TROWEL, NOTCH TROWEL Metal rectangular tool with a handle that is used to comb and spread thinset adhesive. It has notches on two ends and flat edges on the others.

V-CAP An L- or 7-shaped tile with a raised edge at its upper curve. A trim piece often used for kitchen countertops.

VITREOUS Dense-bodied tile that absorbs little or no water.

WATERPROOFING OR ANTIFRACTURE MEMBRANE A slip sheet or paste substance that allows for some movement of the substrate. Tile adhesive is applied to the surface of the membrane.

INDEX